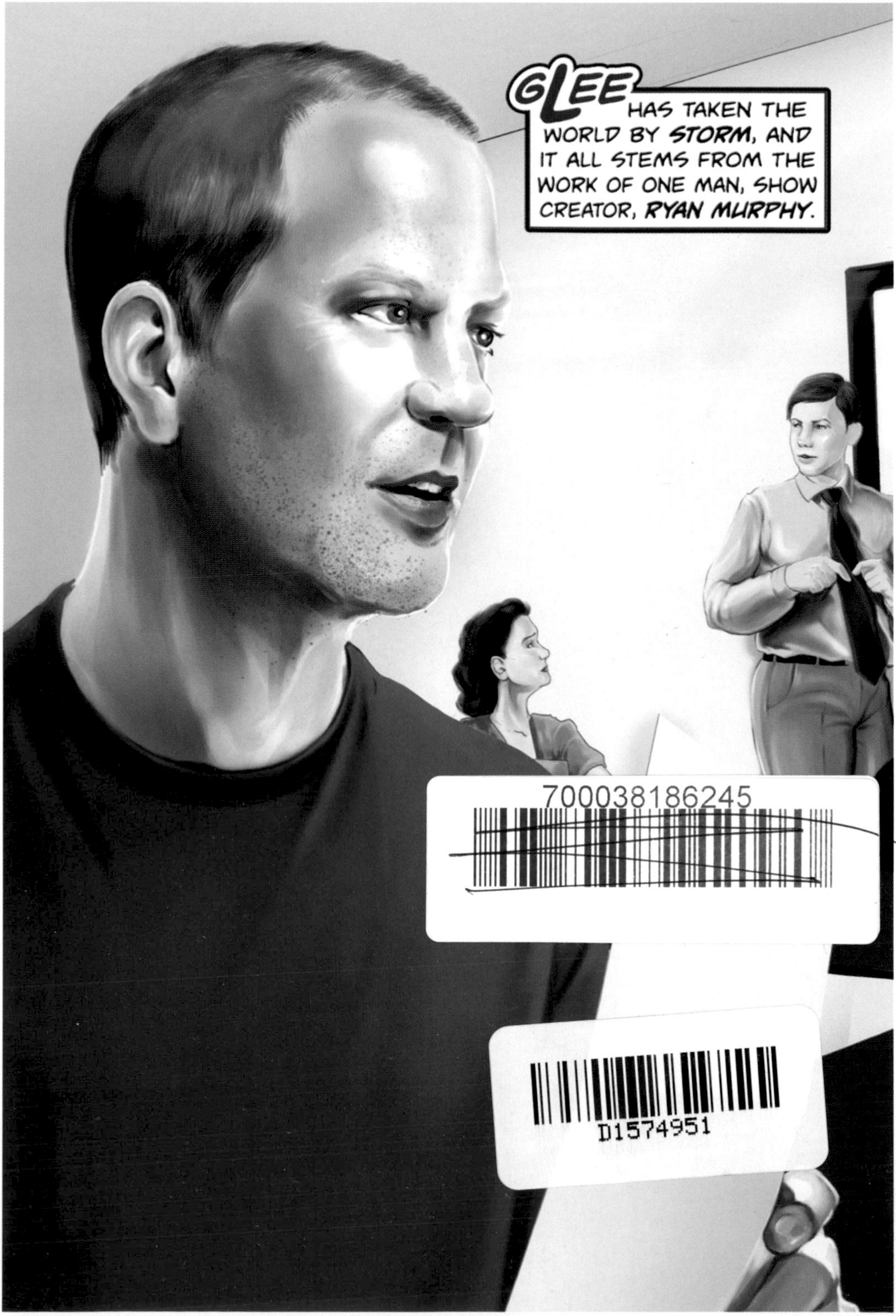
GLEE HAS TAKEN THE WORLD BY STORM, AND IT ALL STEMS FROM THE WORK OF ONE MAN, SHOW CREATOR, RYAN MURPHY.

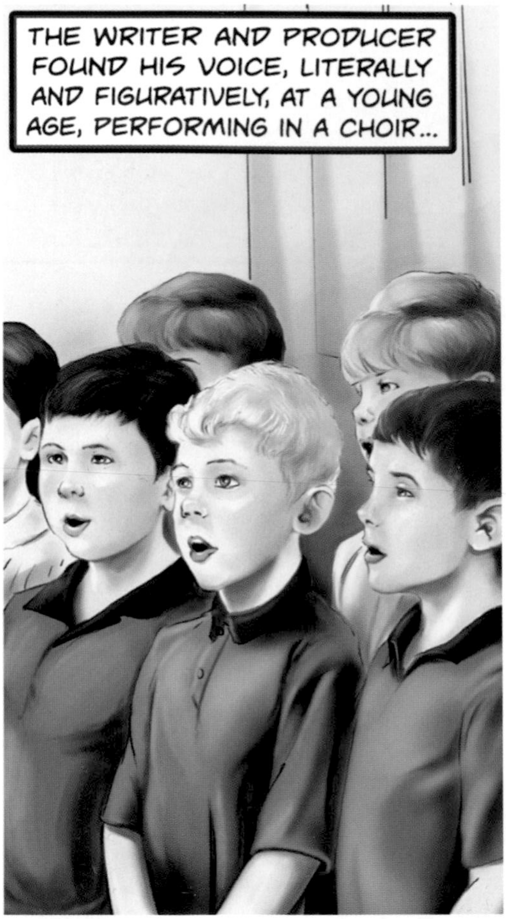
THE WRITER AND PRODUCER FOUND HIS VOICE, LITERALLY AND FIGURATIVELY, AT A YOUNG AGE, PERFORMING IN A CHOIR...

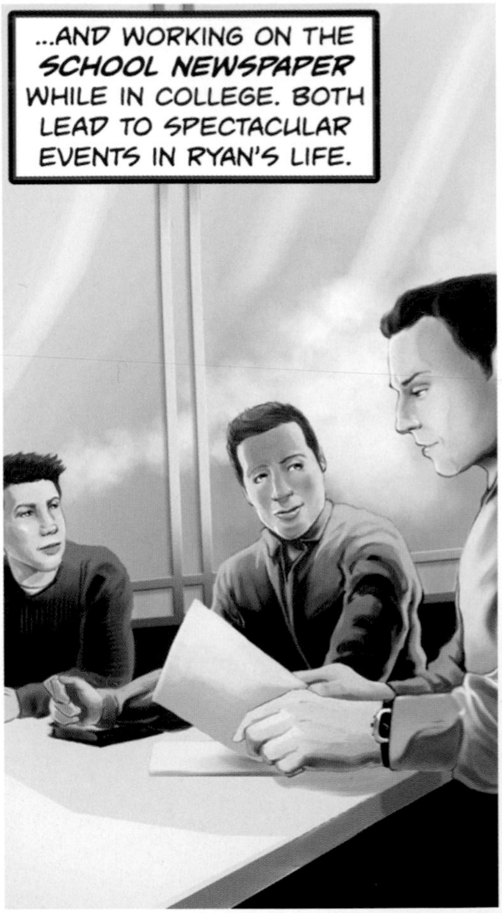
...AND WORKING ON THE *SCHOOL NEWSPAPER* WHILE IN COLLEGE. BOTH LEAD TO SPECTACULAR EVENTS IN RYAN'S LIFE.

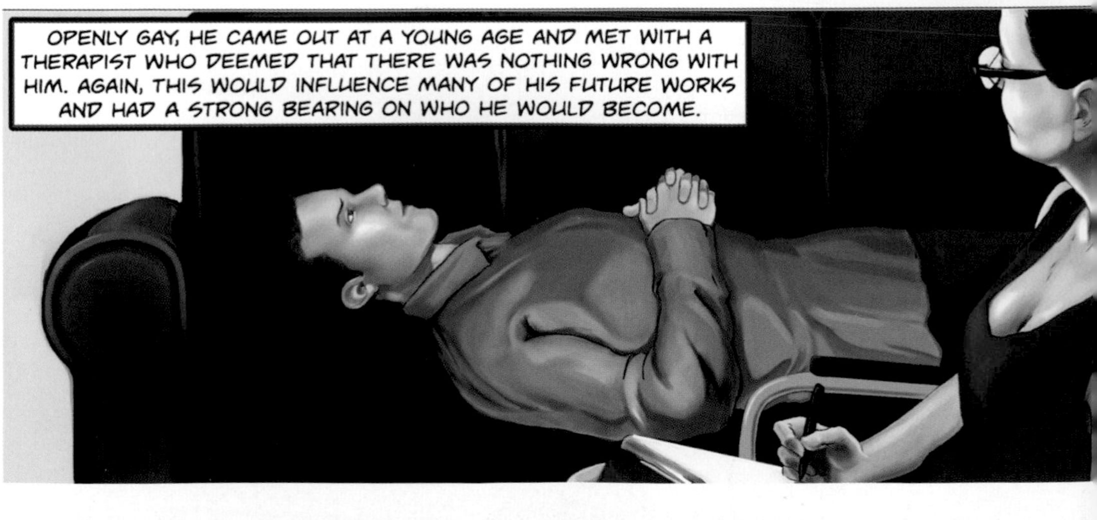
OPENLY GAY, HE CAME OUT AT A YOUNG AGE AND MET WITH A THERAPIST WHO DEEMED THAT THERE WAS NOTHING WRONG WITH HIM. AGAIN, THIS WOULD INFLUENCE MANY OF HIS FUTURE WORKS AND HAD A STRONG BEARING ON WHO HE WOULD BECOME.

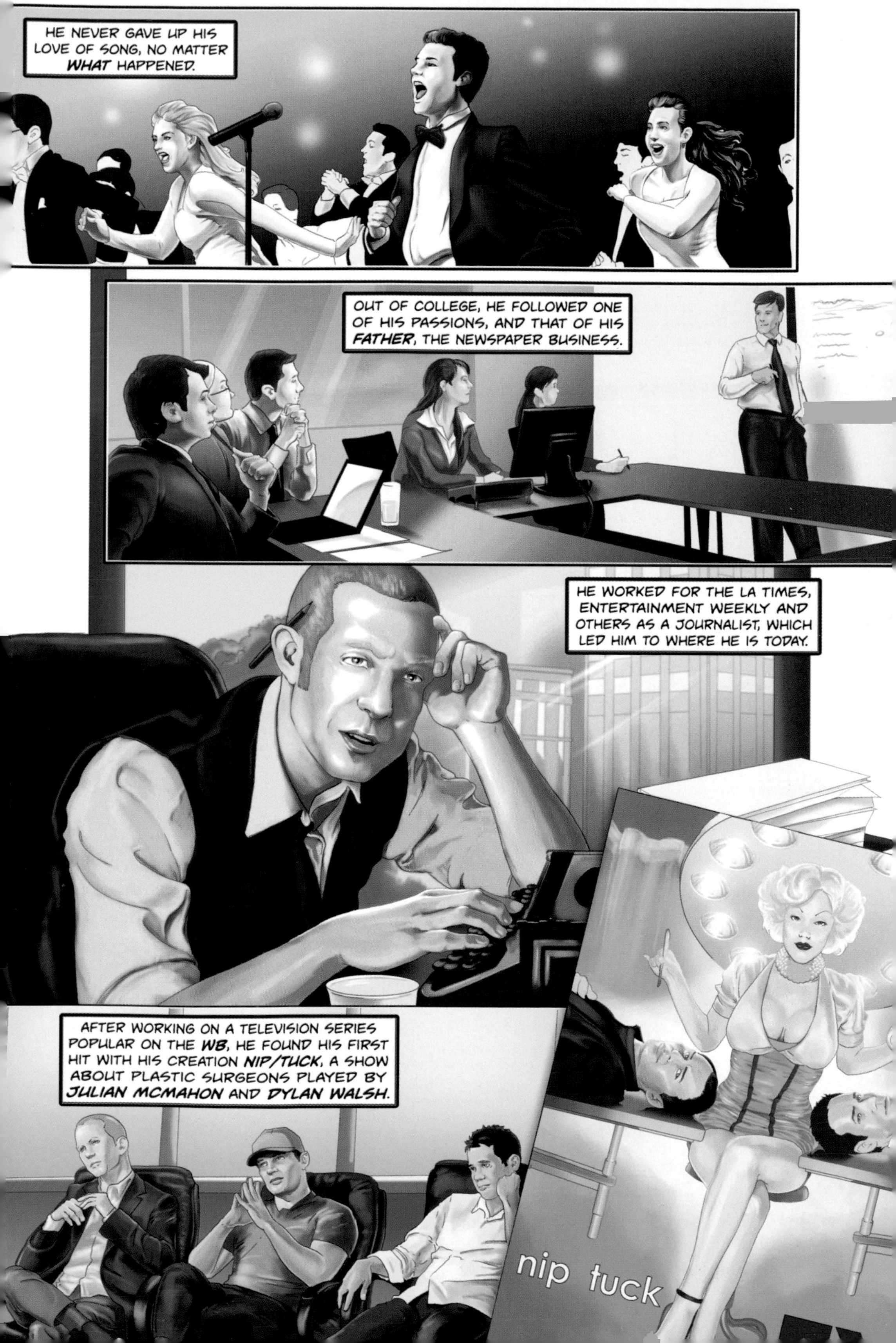

HE NEVER GAVE UP HIS LOVE OF SONG, NO MATTER WHAT HAPPENED.
OUT OF COLLEGE, HE FOLLOWED ONE OF HIS PASSIONS, AND THAT OF HIS FATHER, THE NEWSPAPER BUSINESS.
HE WORKED FOR THE LA TIMES, ENTERTAINMENT WEEKLY AND OTHERS AS A JOURNALIST, WHICH LED HIM TO WHERE HE IS TODAY.
AFTER WORKING ON A TELEVISION SERIES POPULAR ON THE WB, HE FOUND HIS FIRST HIT WITH HIS CREATION NIP/TUCK, A SHOW ABOUT PLASTIC SURGEONS PLAYED BY JULIAN MCMAHON AND DYLAN WALSH.
nip tuck

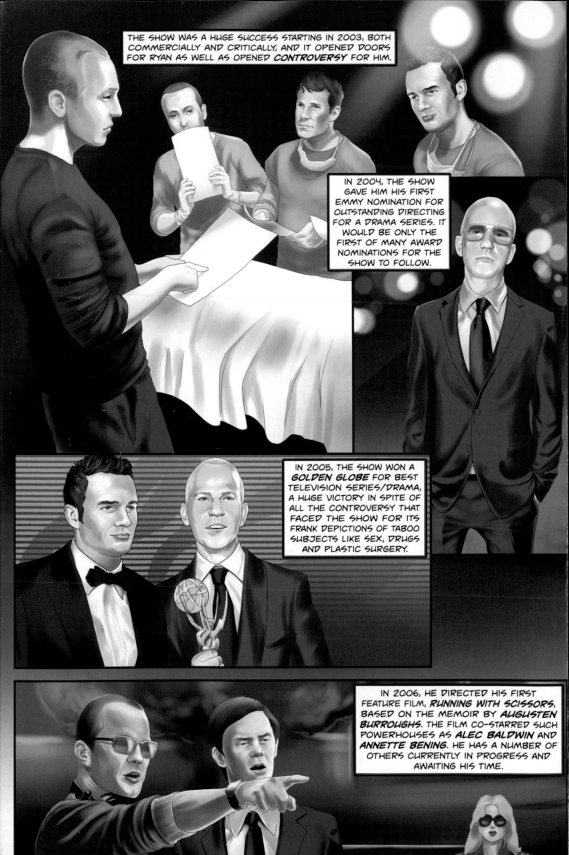

THE SHOW WAS A HUGE SUCCESS STARTING IN 2003, BOTH COMMERCIALLY AND CRITICALLY, AND IT OPENED DOORS FOR RYAN AS WELL AS OPENED **CONTROVERSY** FOR HIM.

IN 2004, THE SHOW GAVE HIM HIS FIRST EMMY NOMINATION FOR OUTSTANDING DIRECTING FOR A DRAMA SERIES. IT WOULD BE ONLY THE FIRST OF MANY AWARD NOMINATIONS FOR THE SHOW TO FOLLOW.

IN 2005, THE SHOW WON A **GOLDEN GLOBE** FOR BEST TELEVISION SERIES/DRAMA, A HUGE VICTORY IN SPITE OF ALL THE CONTROVERSY THAT FACED THE SHOW FOR ITS FRANK DEPICTIONS OF TABOO SUBJECTS LIKE SEX, DRUGS AND PLASTIC SURGERY.

IN 2006, HE DIRECTED HIS FIRST FEATURE FILM, **RUNNING WITH SCISSORS,** BASED ON THE MEMOIR BY **AUGUSTEN BURROUGHS.** THE FILM CO-STARRED SUCH POWERHOUSES AS **ALEC BALDWIN** AND **ANNETTE BENING.** HE HAS A NUMBER OF OTHERS CURRENTLY IN PROGRESS AND AWAITING HIS TIME.

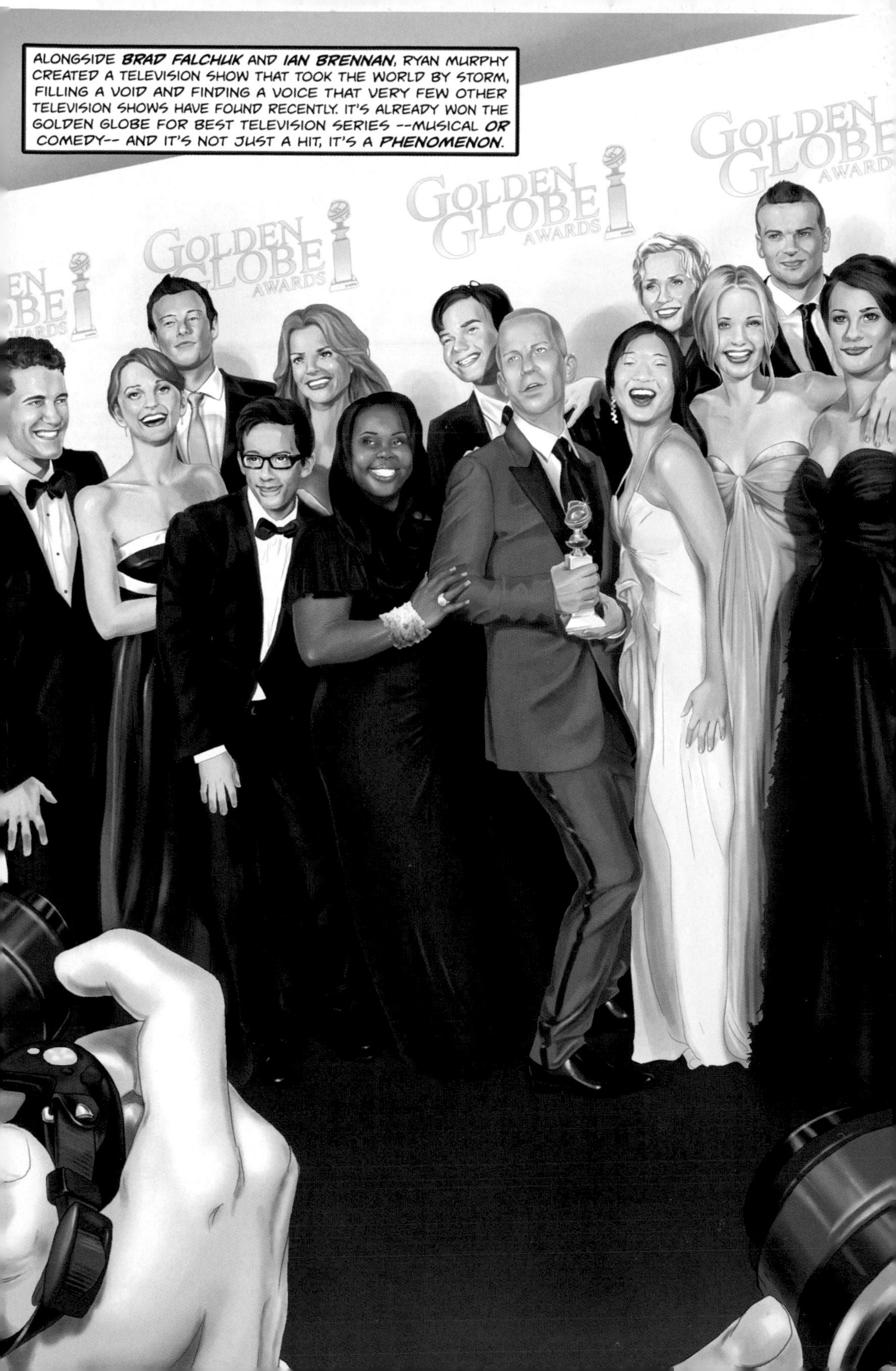
ALONGSIDE BRAD FALCHUK AND IAN BRENNAN, RYAN MURPHY CREATED A TELEVISION SHOW THAT TOOK THE WORLD BY STORM, FILLING A VOID AND FINDING A VOICE THAT VERY FEW OTHER TELEVISION SHOWS HAVE FOUND RECENTLY. IT'S ALREADY WON THE GOLDEN GLOBE FOR BEST TELEVISION SERIES --MUSICAL OR COMEDY-- AND IT'S NOT JUST A HIT, IT'S A PHENOMENON.
GOLDEN GLOBE AWARDS

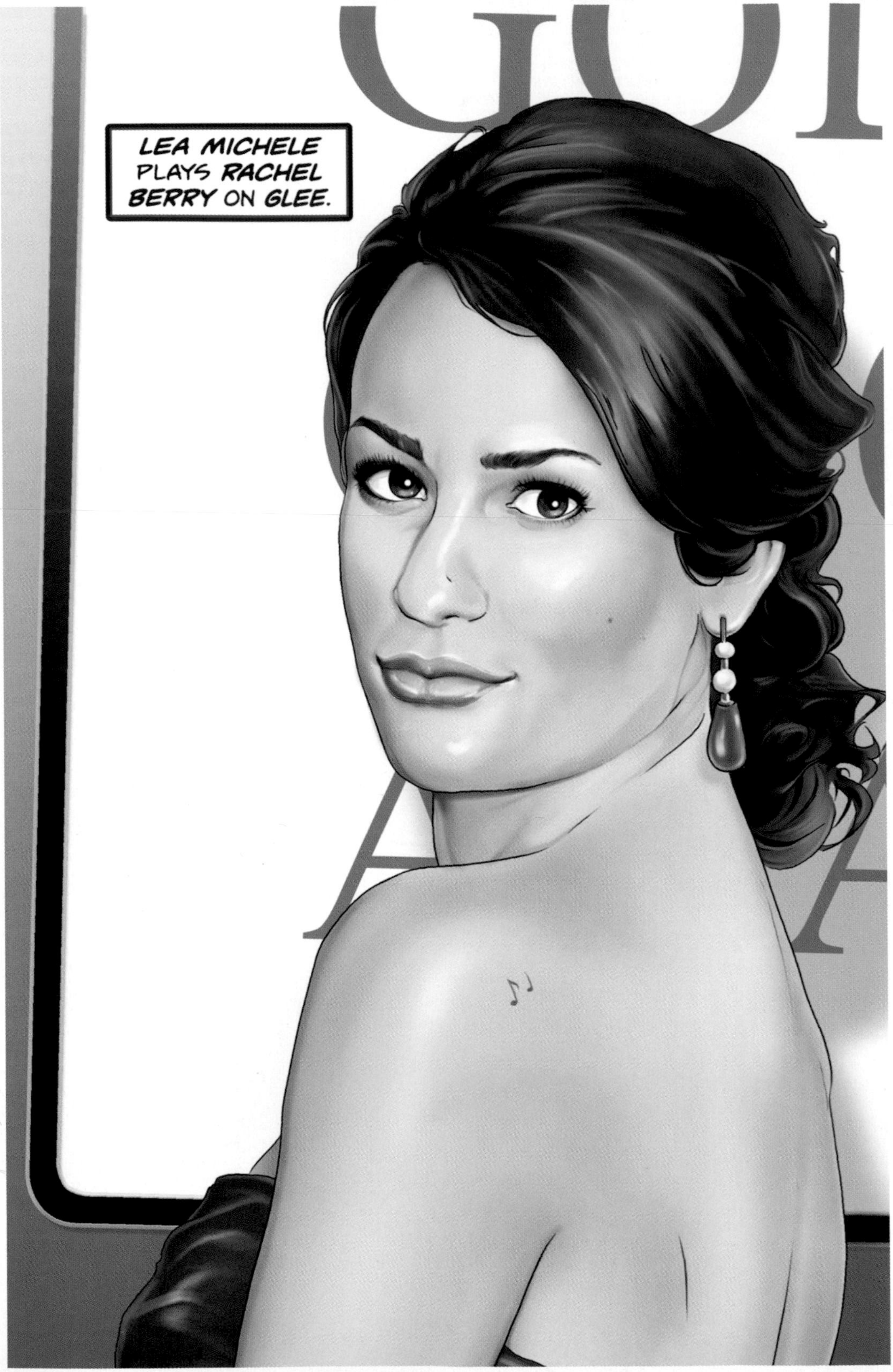
LEA MICHELE PLAYS RACHEL BERRY ON GLEE.

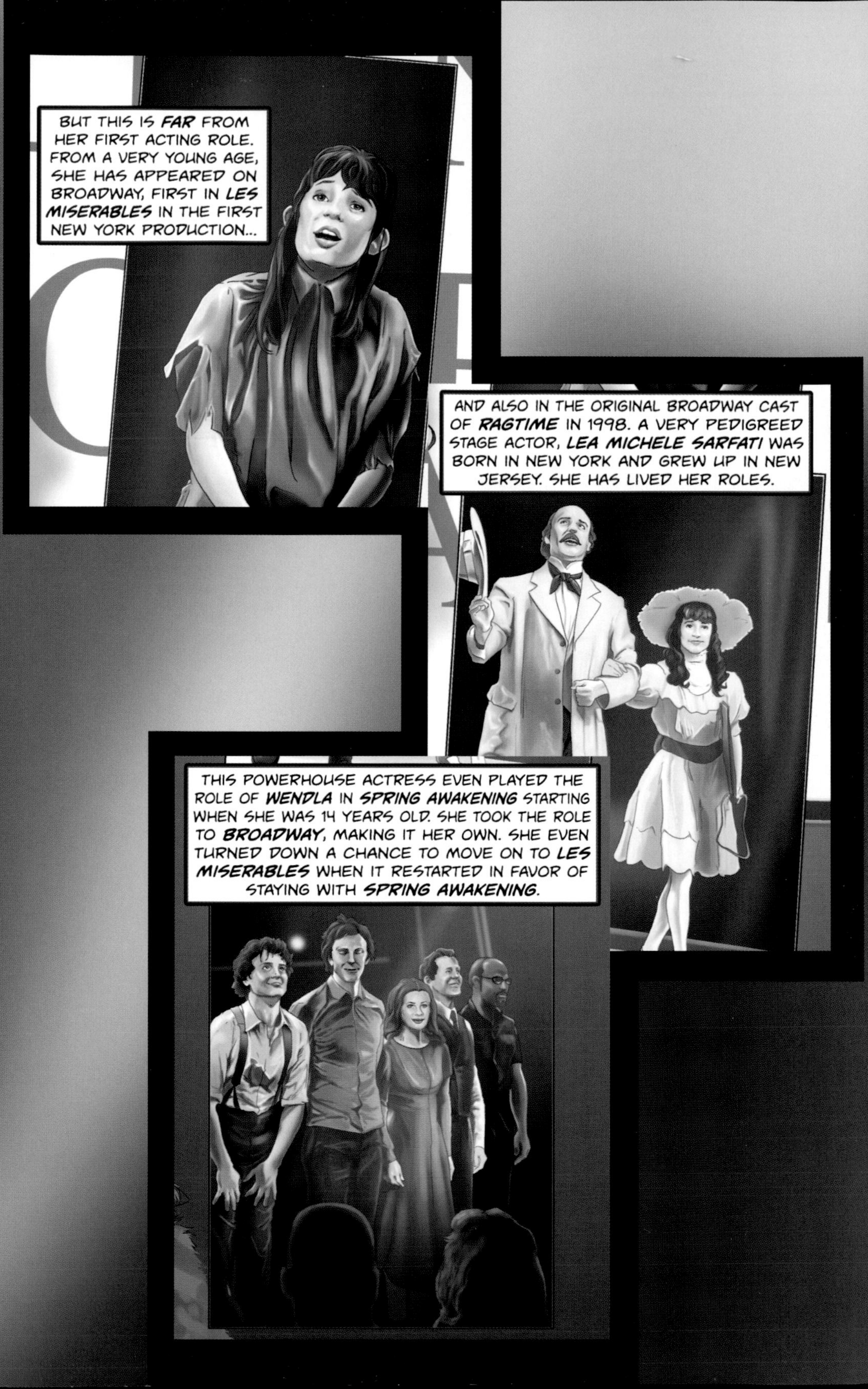
BUT THIS IS FAR FROM HER FIRST ACTING ROLE. FROM A VERY YOUNG AGE, SHE HAS APPEARED ON BROADWAY, FIRST IN LES MISERABLES IN THE FIRST NEW YORK PRODUCTION...
AND ALSO IN THE ORIGINAL BROADWAY CAST OF RAGTIME IN 1998. A VERY PEDIGREED STAGE ACTOR, LEA MICHELE SARFATI WAS BORN IN NEW YORK AND GREW UP IN NEW JERSEY. SHE HAS LIVED HER ROLES.
THIS POWERHOUSE ACTRESS EVEN PLAYED THE ROLE OF WENDLA IN SPRING AWAKENING STARTING WHEN SHE WAS 14 YEARS OLD. SHE TOOK THE ROLE TO BROADWAY, MAKING IT HER OWN. SHE EVEN TURNED DOWN A CHANCE TO MOVE ON TO LES MISERABLES WHEN IT RESTARTED IN FAVOR OF STAYING WITH SPRING AWAKENING.

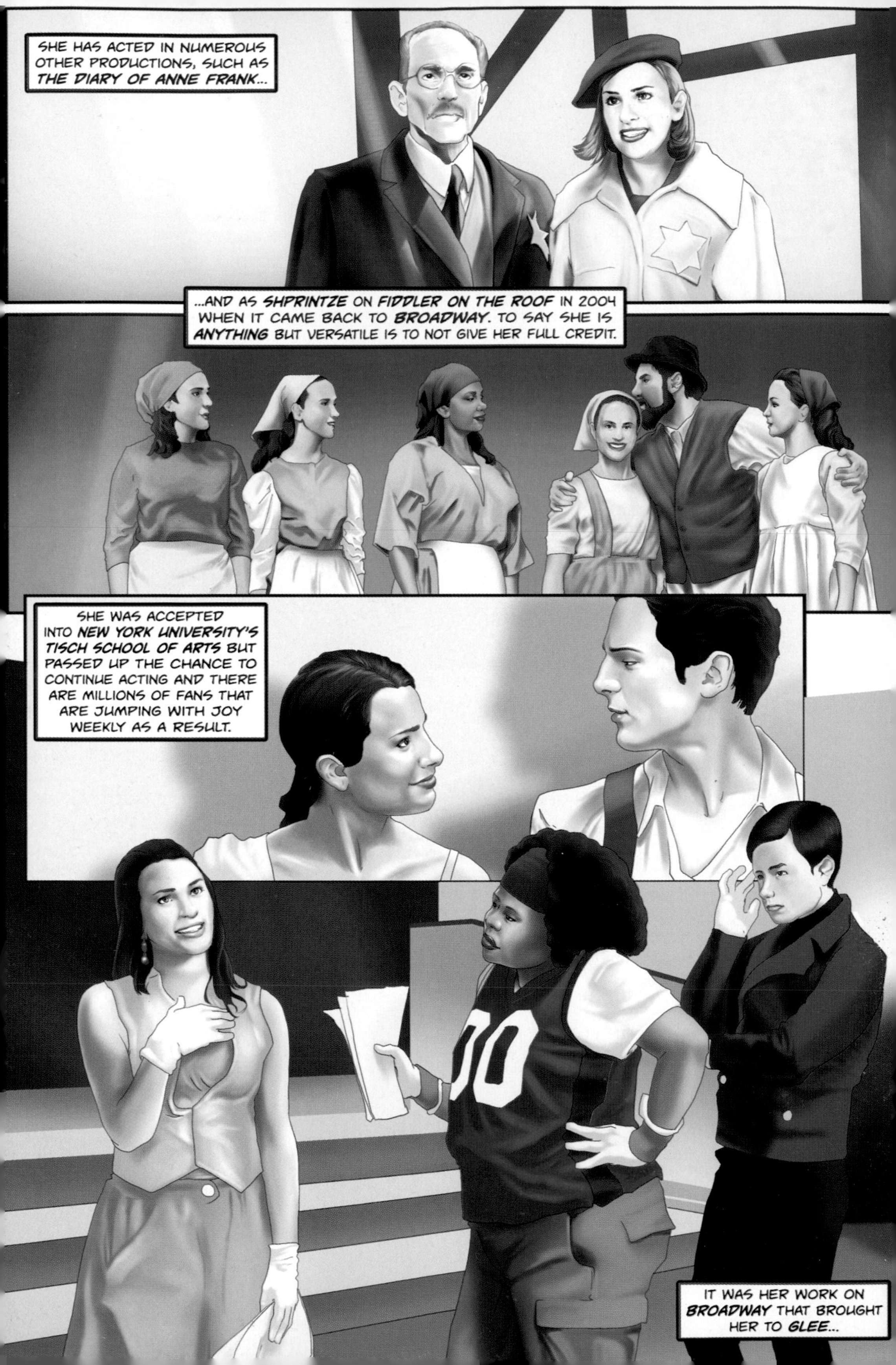
SHE HAS ACTED IN NUMEROUS OTHER PRODUCTIONS, SUCH AS THE DIARY OF ANNE FRANK...
...AND AS SHPRINTZE ON FIDDLER ON THE ROOF IN 2004 WHEN IT CAME BACK TO BROADWAY. TO SAY SHE IS ANYTHING BUT VERSATILE IS TO NOT GIVE HER FULL CREDIT.
SHE WAS ACCEPTED INTO NEW YORK UNIVERSITY'S TISCH SCHOOL OF ARTS BUT PASSED UP THE CHANCE TO CONTINUE ACTING AND THERE ARE MILLIONS OF FANS THAT ARE JUMPING WITH JOY WEEKLY AS A RESULT.
00
IT WAS HER WORK ON BROADWAY THAT BROUGHT HER TO GLEE...

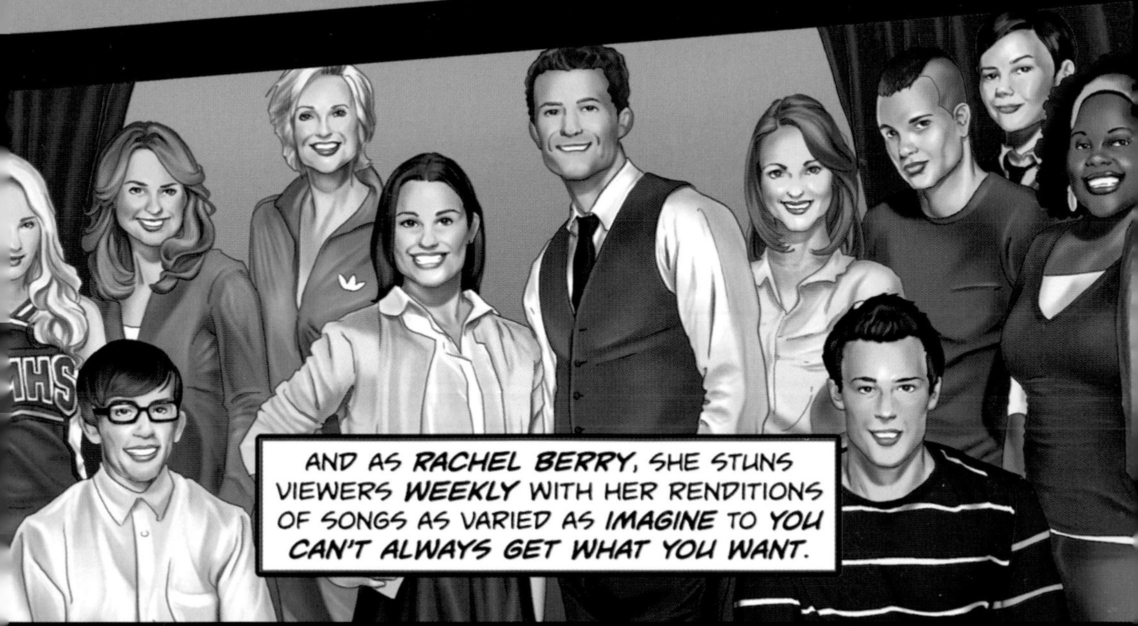
AND AS RACHEL BERRY, SHE STUNS VIEWERS WEEKLY WITH HER RENDITIONS OF SONGS AS VARIED AS IMAGINE TO YOU CAN'T ALWAYS GET WHAT YOU WANT.

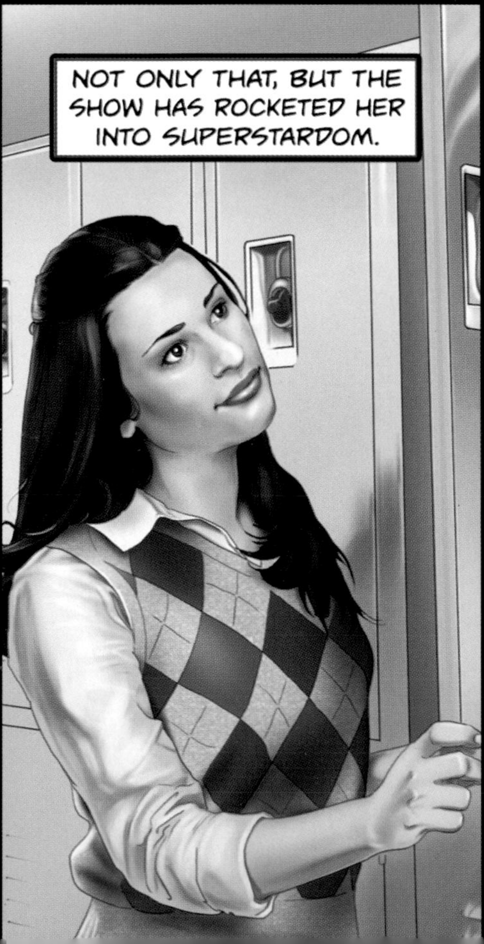
NOT ONLY THAT, BUT THE SHOW HAS ROCKETED HER INTO SUPERSTARDOM.

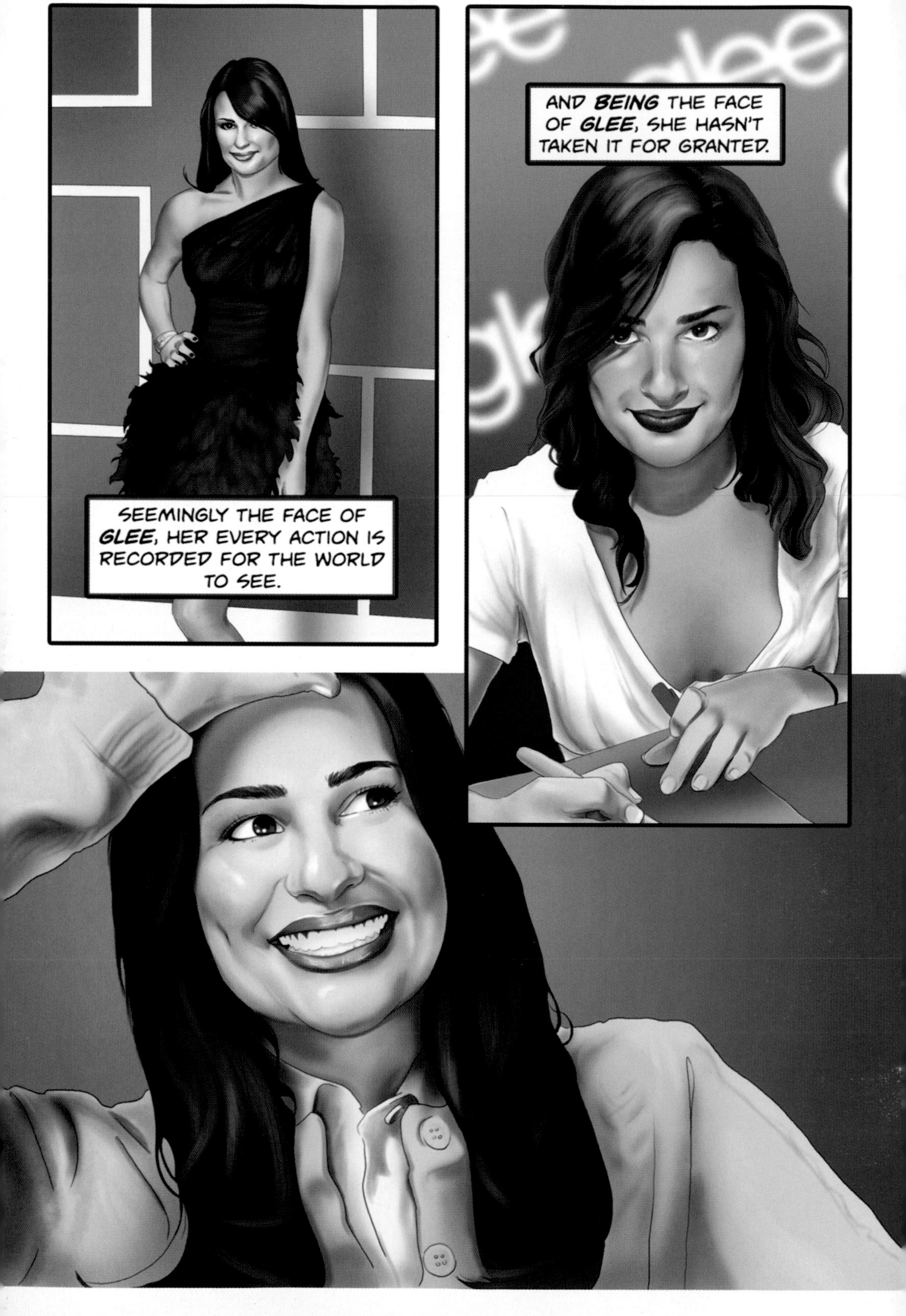
SEEMINGLY THE FACE OF GLEE, HER EVERY ACTION IS RECORDED FOR THE WORLD TO SEE.
AND BEING THE FACE OF GLEE, SHE HASN'T TAKEN IT FOR GRANTED.

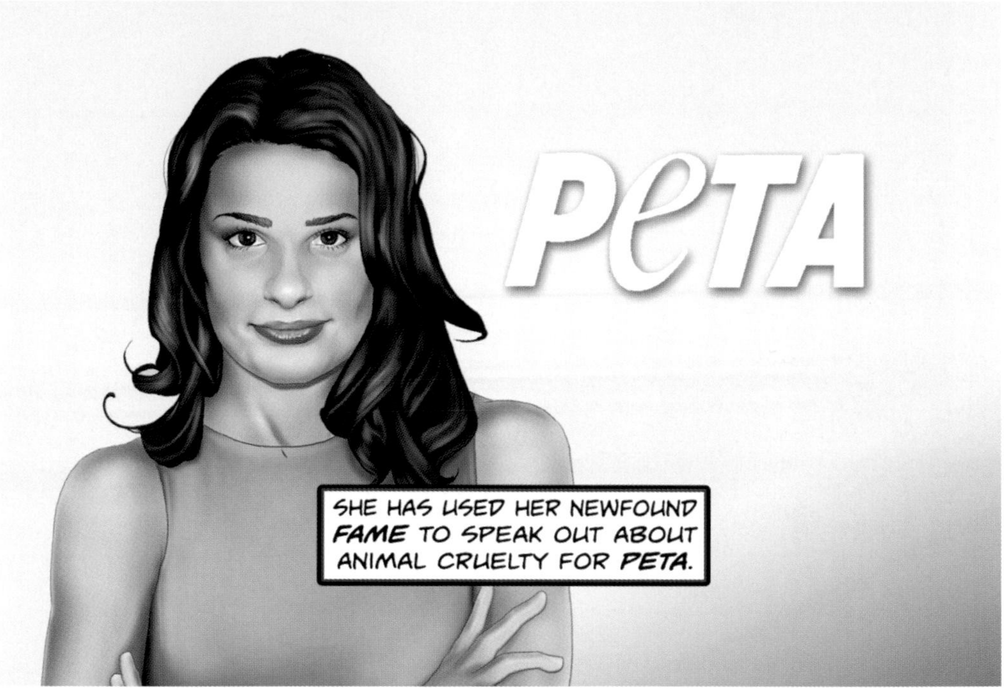
PETA
SHE HAS USED HER NEWFOUND FAME TO SPEAK OUT ABOUT ANIMAL CRUELTY FOR PETA.

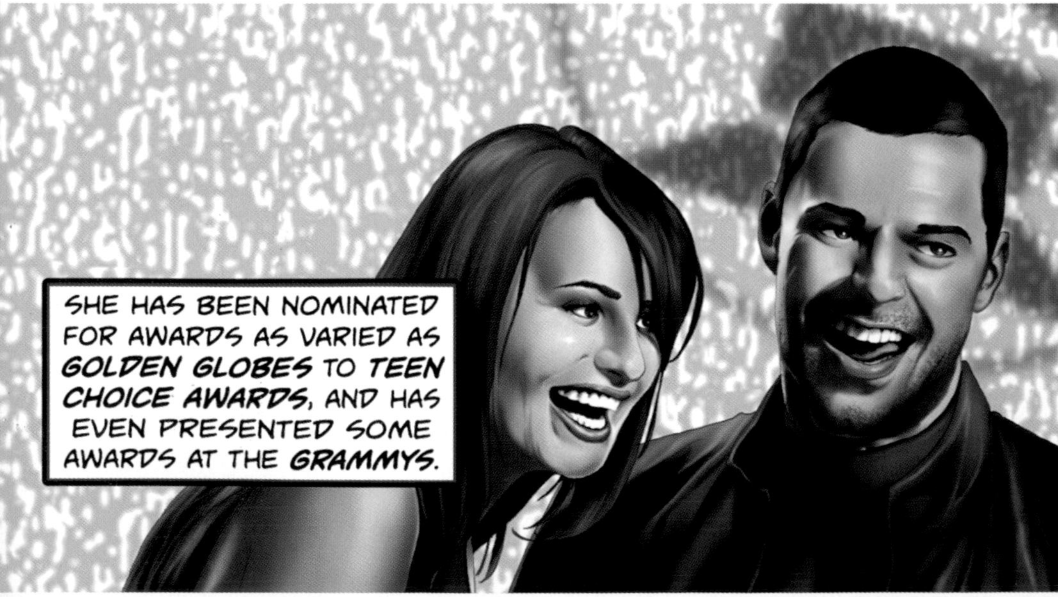
SHE HAS BEEN NOMINATED FOR AWARDS AS VARIED AS GOLDEN GLOBES TO TEEN CHOICE AWARDS, AND HAS EVEN PRESENTED SOME AWARDS AT THE GRAMMYS.

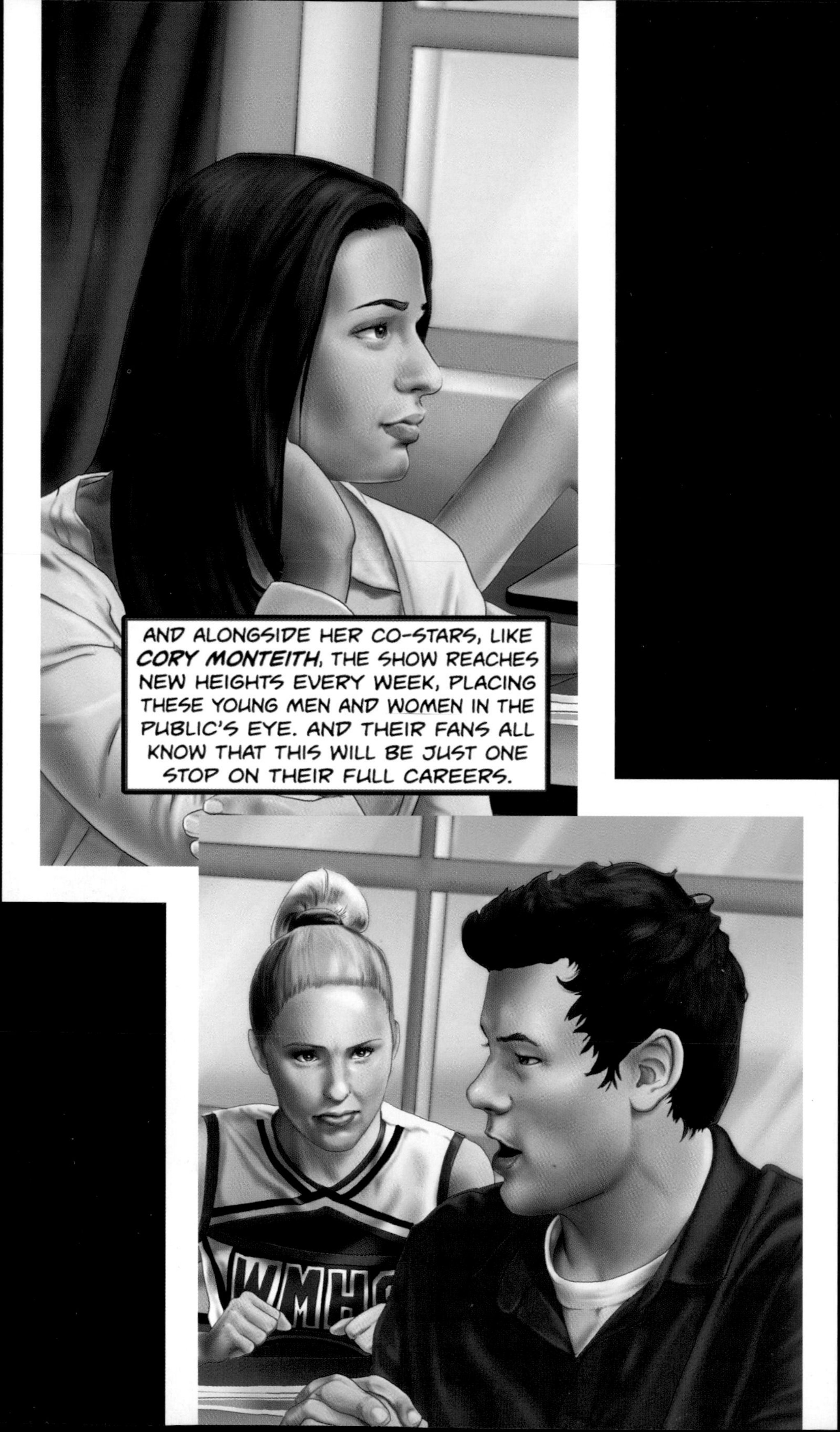
AND ALONGSIDE HER CO-STARS, LIKE CORY MONTEITH, THE SHOW REACHES NEW HEIGHTS EVERY WEEK, PLACING THESE YOUNG MEN AND WOMEN IN THE PUBLIC'S EYE. AND THEIR FANS ALL KNOW THAT THIS WILL BE JUST ONE STOP ON THEIR FULL CAREERS.
WMHS

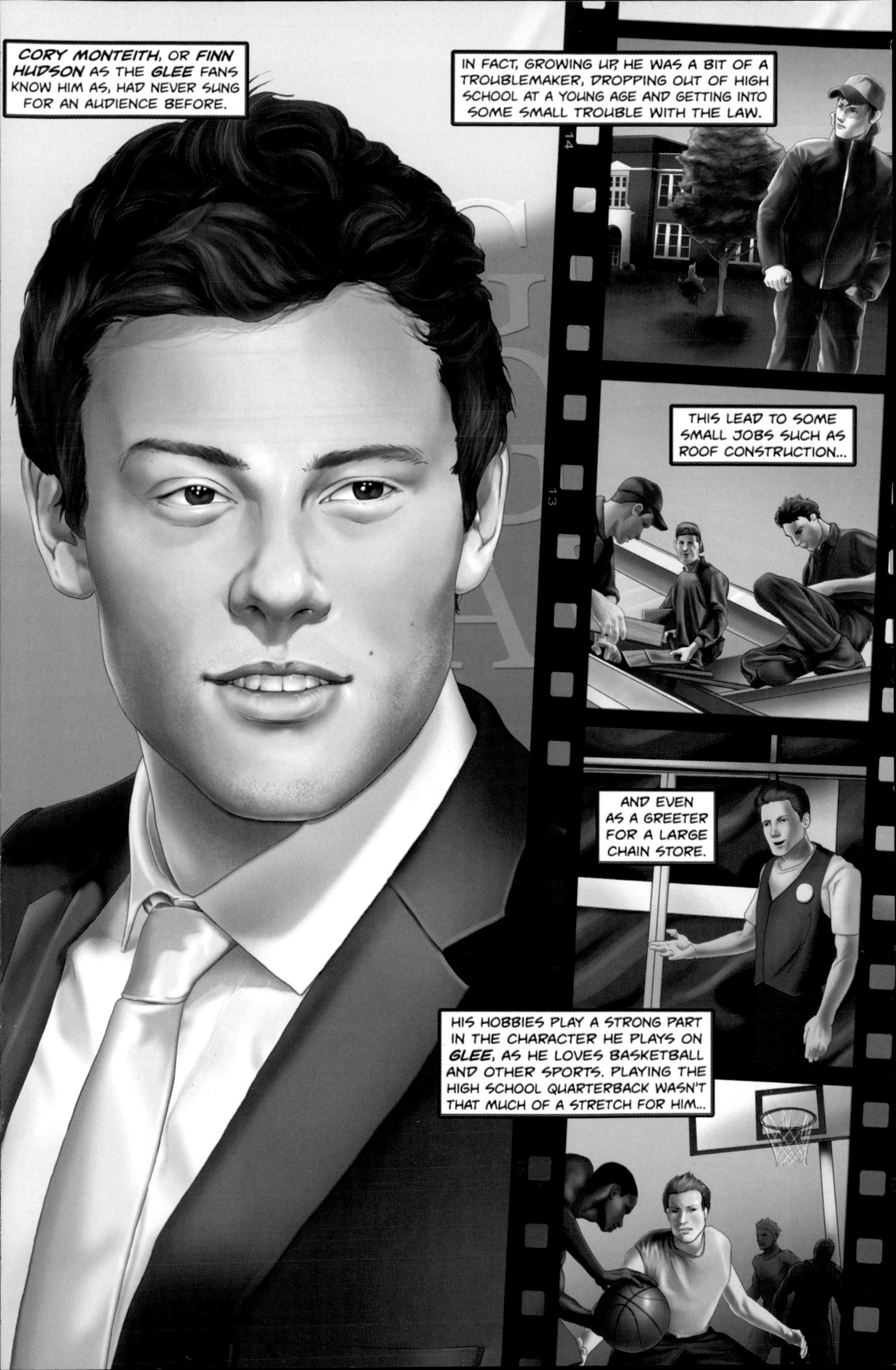
CORY MONTEITH, OR FINN HUDSON AS THE GLEE FANS KNOW HIM AS, HAD NEVER SUNG FOR AN AUDIENCE BEFORE.
IN FACT, GROWING UP, HE WAS A BIT OF A TROUBLEMAKER, DROPPING OUT OF HIGH SCHOOL AT A YOUNG AGE AND GETTING INTO SOME SMALL TROUBLE WITH THE LAW.
THIS LEAD TO SOME SMALL JOBS SUCH AS ROOF CONSTRUCTION...
AND EVEN AS A GREETER FOR A LARGE CHAIN STORE.
HIS HOBBIES PLAY A STRONG PART IN THE CHARACTER HE PLAYS ON GLEE, AS HE LOVES BASKETBALL AND OTHER SPORTS. PLAYING THE HIGH SCHOOL QUARTERBACK WASN'T THAT MUCH OF A STRETCH FOR HIM...

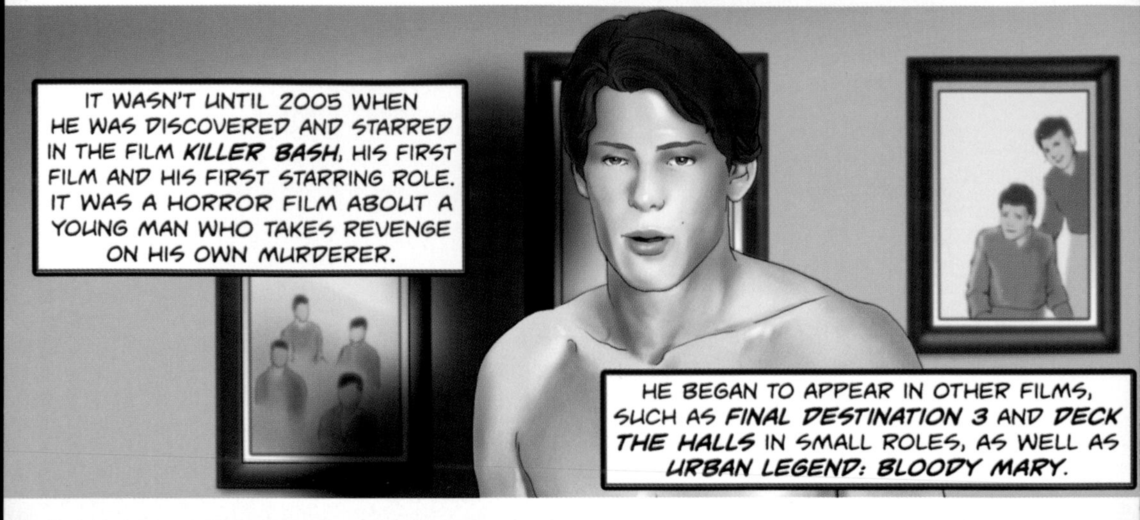
IT WASN'T UNTIL 2005 WHEN HE WAS DISCOVERED AND STARRED IN THE FILM KILLER BASH, HIS FIRST FILM AND HIS FIRST STARRING ROLE. IT WAS A HORROR FILM ABOUT A YOUNG MAN WHO TAKES REVENGE ON HIS OWN MURDERER.
HE BEGAN TO APPEAR IN OTHER FILMS, SUCH AS FINAL DESTINATION 3 AND DECK THE HALLS IN SMALL ROLES, AS WELL AS URBAN LEGEND: BLOODY MARY.

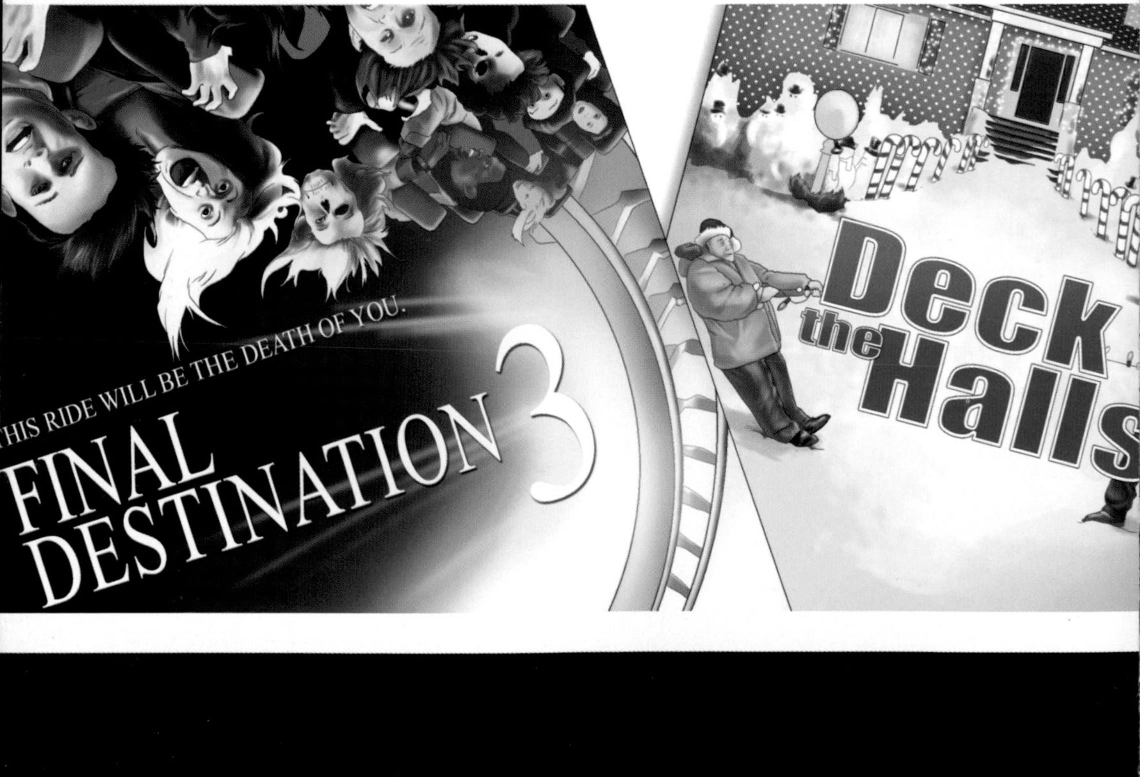
THIS RIDE WILL BE THE DEATH OF YOU.
FINAL DESTINATION 3
Deck the Halls

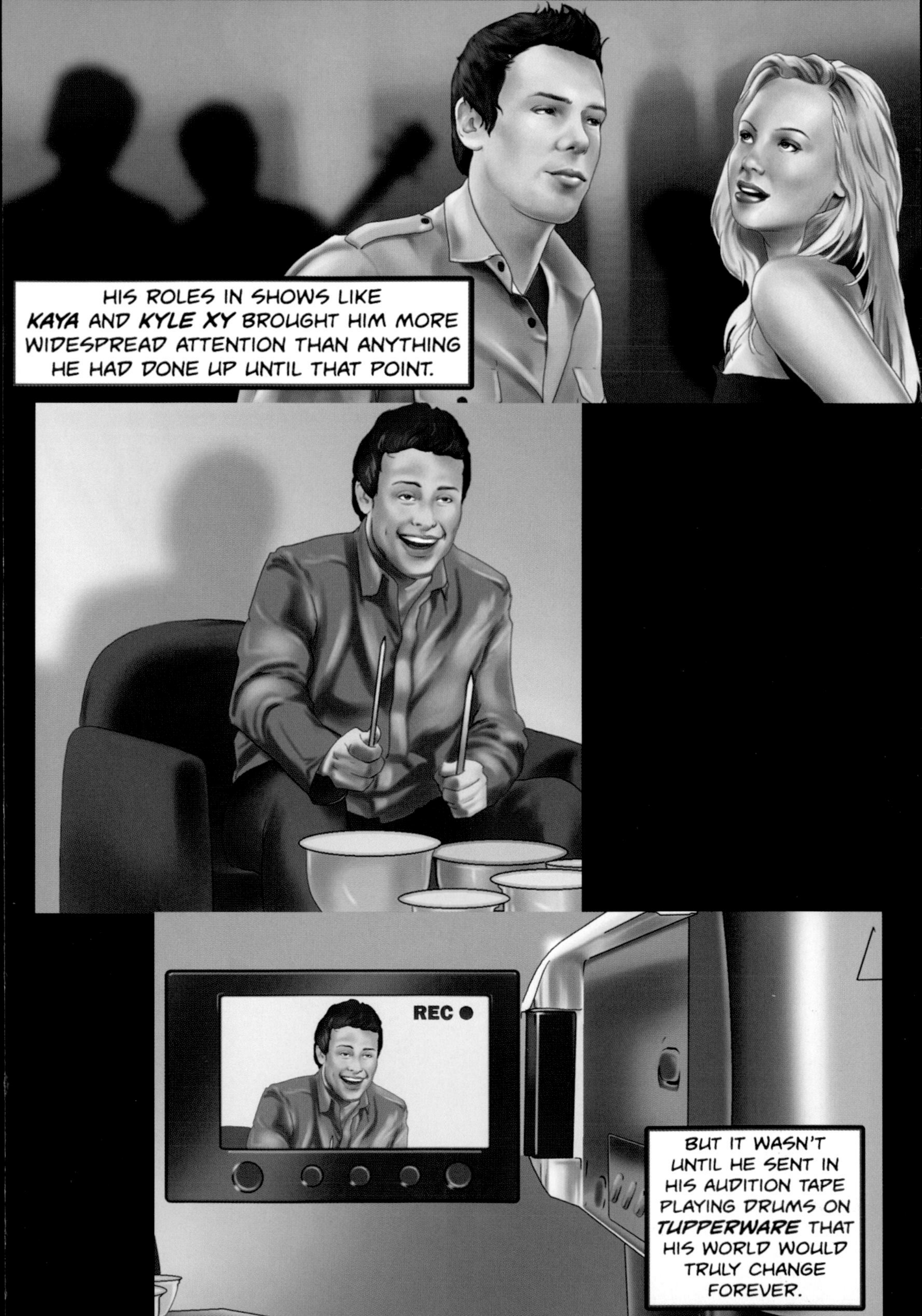
HIS ROLES IN SHOWS LIKE KAYA AND KYLE XY BROUGHT HIM MORE WIDESPREAD ATTENTION THAN ANYTHING HE HAD DONE UP UNTIL THAT POINT.
REC
BUT IT WASN'T UNTIL HE SENT IN HIS AUDITION TAPE PLAYING DRUMS ON TUPPERWARE THAT HIS WORLD WOULD TRULY CHANGE FOREVER.

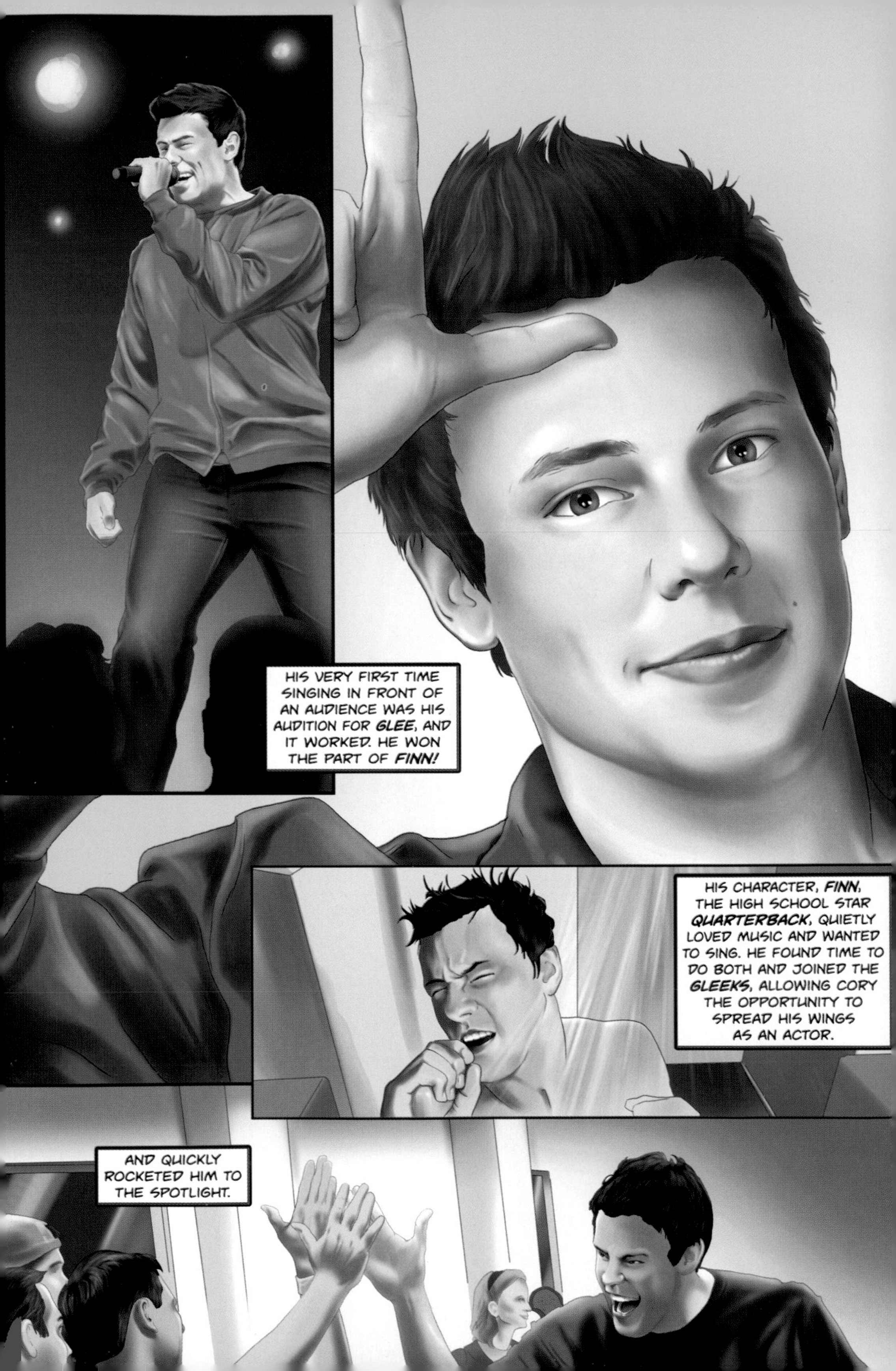
HIS VERY FIRST TIME SINGING IN FRONT OF AN AUDIENCE WAS HIS AUDITION FOR GLEE, AND IT WORKED. HE WON THE PART OF FINN!
HIS CHARACTER, FINN, THE HIGH SCHOOL STAR QUARTERBACK, QUIETLY LOVED MUSIC AND WANTED TO SING. HE FOUND TIME TO DO BOTH AND JOINED THE GLEEKS, ALLOWING CORY THE OPPORTUNITY TO SPREAD HIS WINGS AS AN ACTOR.
AND QUICKLY ROCKETED HIM TO THE SPOTLIGHT.

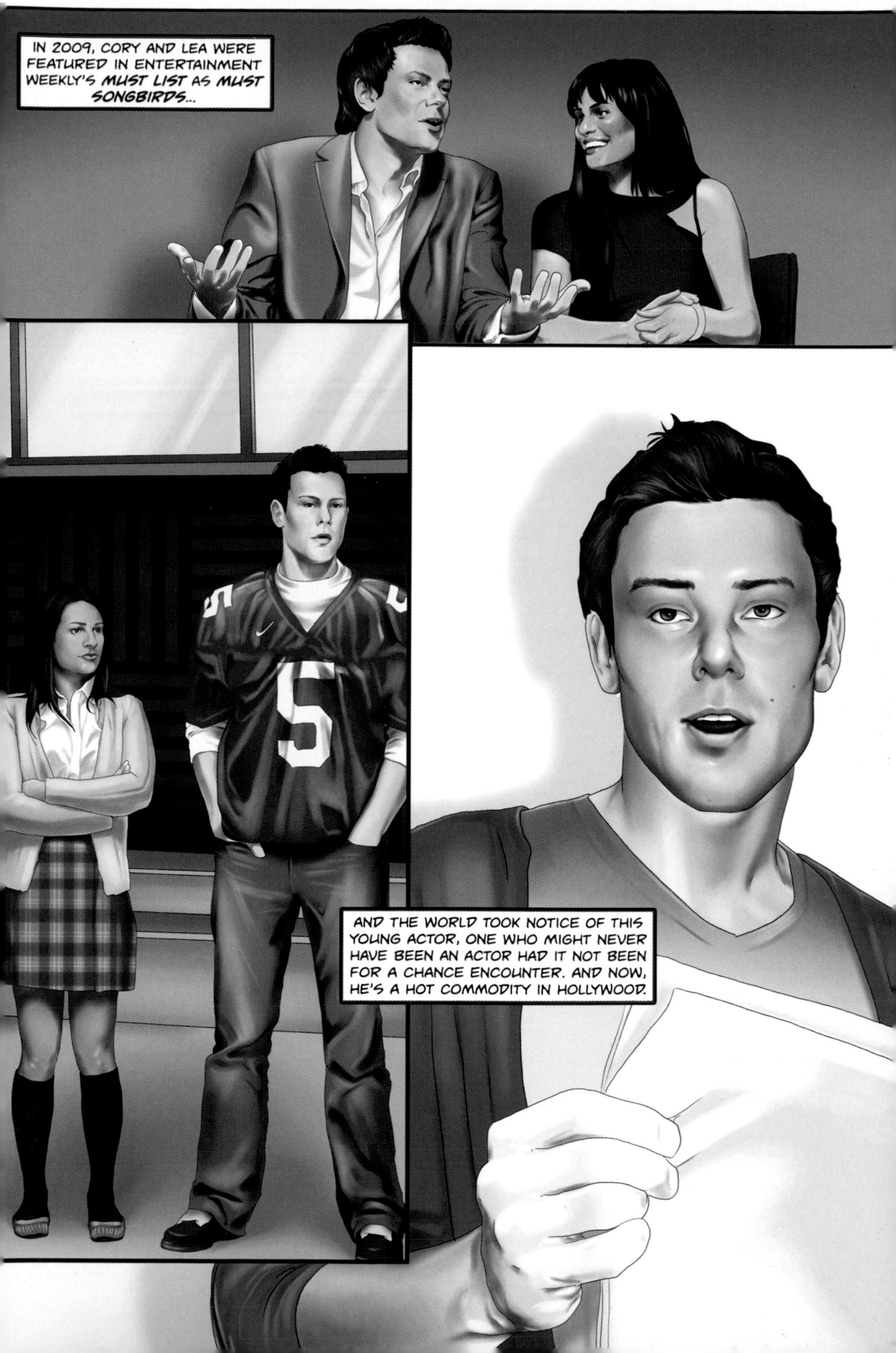
IN 2009, CORY AND LEA WERE FEATURED IN ENTERTAINMENT WEEKLY'S MUST LIST AS MUST SONGBIRDS...
5
5
AND THE WORLD TOOK NOTICE OF THIS YOUNG ACTOR, ONE WHO MIGHT NEVER HAVE BEEN AN ACTOR HAD IT NOT BEEN FOR A CHANCE ENCOUNTER. AND NOW, HE'S A HOT COMMODITY IN HOLLYWOOD.

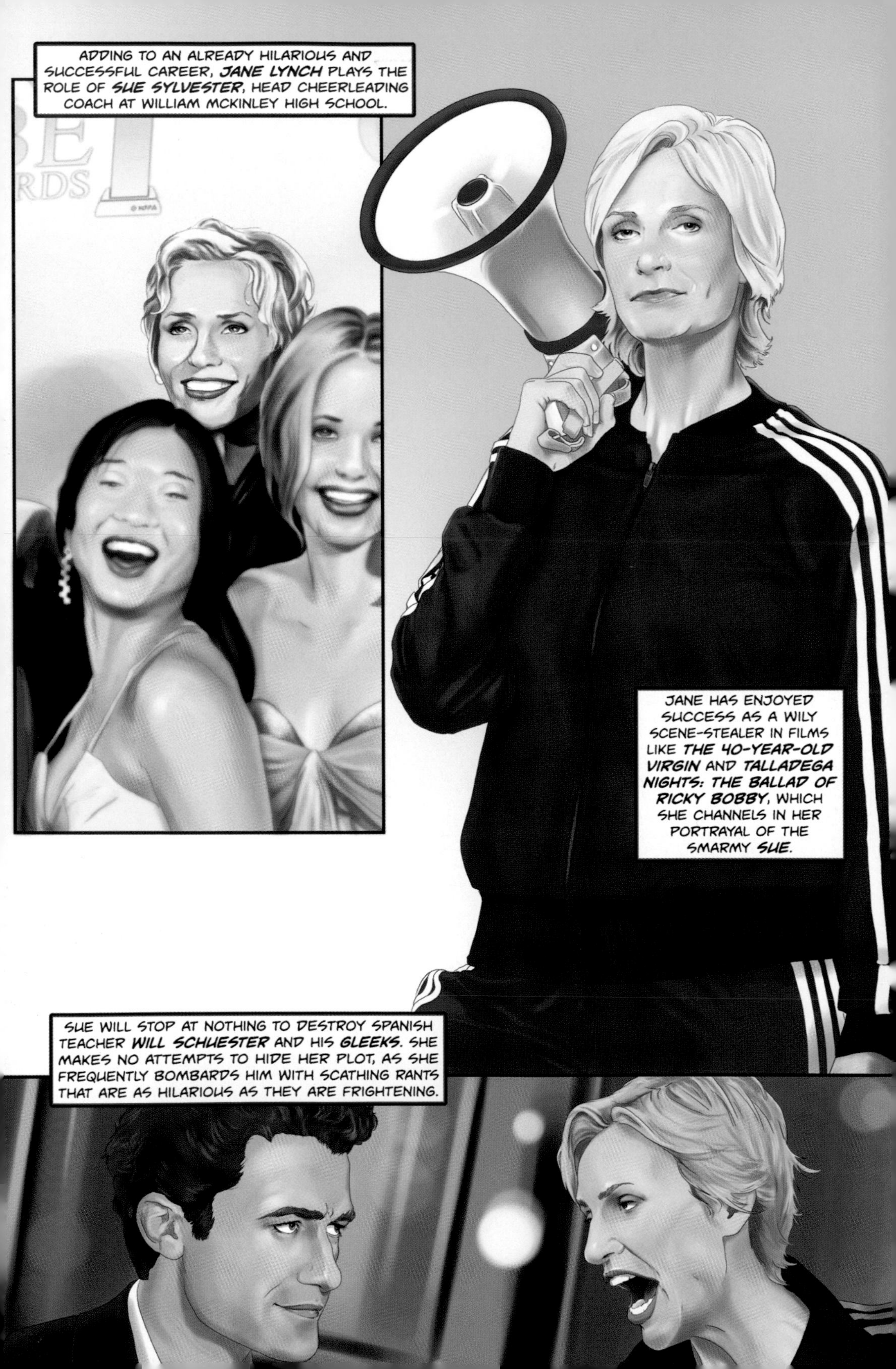
ADDING TO AN ALREADY HILARIOUS AND SUCCESSFUL CAREER, ***JANE LYNCH*** PLAYS THE ROLE OF ***SUE SYLVESTER***, HEAD CHEERLEADING COACH AT WILLIAM MCKINLEY HIGH SCHOOL.
JANE HAS ENJOYED SUCCESS AS A WILY SCENE-STEALER IN FILMS LIKE ***THE 40-YEAR-OLD VIRGIN*** AND ***TALLADEGA NIGHTS: THE BALLAD OF RICKY BOBBY***, WHICH SHE CHANNELS IN HER PORTRAYAL OF THE SMARMY ***SUE***.
SUE WILL STOP AT NOTHING TO DESTROY SPANISH TEACHER ***WILL SCHUESTER*** AND HIS ***GLEEKS***. SHE MAKES NO ATTEMPTS TO HIDE HER PLOT, AS SHE FREQUENTLY BOMBARDS HIM WITH SCATHING RANTS THAT ARE AS HILARIOUS AS THEY ARE FRIGHTENING.

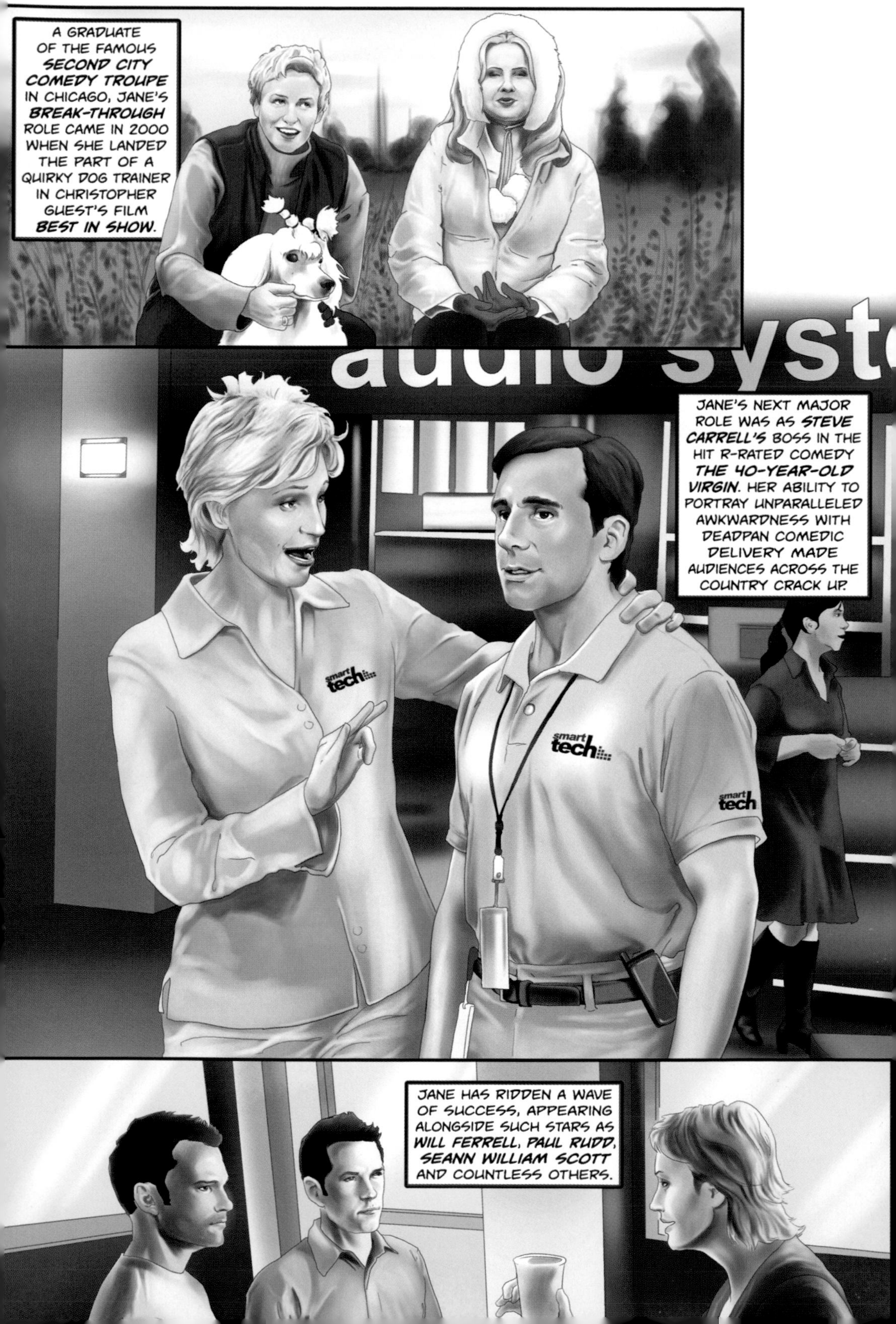
A GRADUATE OF THE FAMOUS SECOND CITY COMEDY TROUPE IN CHICAGO, JANE'S BREAK-THROUGH ROLE CAME IN 2000 WHEN SHE LANDED THE PART OF A QUIRKY DOG TRAINER IN CHRISTOPHER GUEST'S FILM BEST IN SHOW.
audio syst
smart tech
JANE'S NEXT MAJOR ROLE WAS AS STEVE CARRELL'S BOSS IN THE HIT R-RATED COMEDY THE 40-YEAR-OLD VIRGIN. HER ABILITY TO PORTRAY UNPARALLELED AWKWARDNESS WITH DEADPAN COMEDIC DELIVERY MADE AUDIENCES ACROSS THE COUNTRY CRACK UP.
JANE HAS RIDDEN A WAVE OF SUCCESS, APPEARING ALONGSIDE SUCH STARS AS WILL FERRELL, PAUL RUDD, SEANN WILLIAM SCOTT AND COUNTLESS OTHERS.

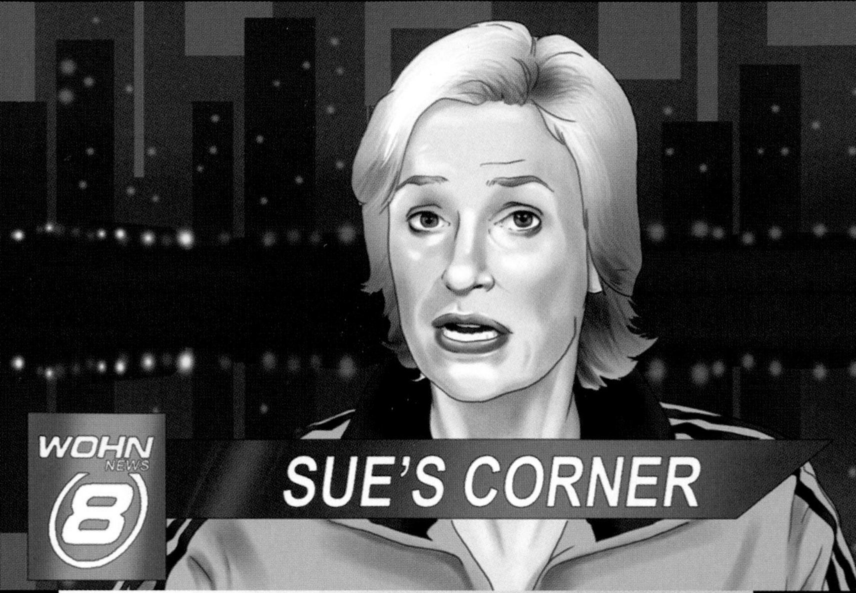
WOHN
NEWS
8
SUE'S CORNER

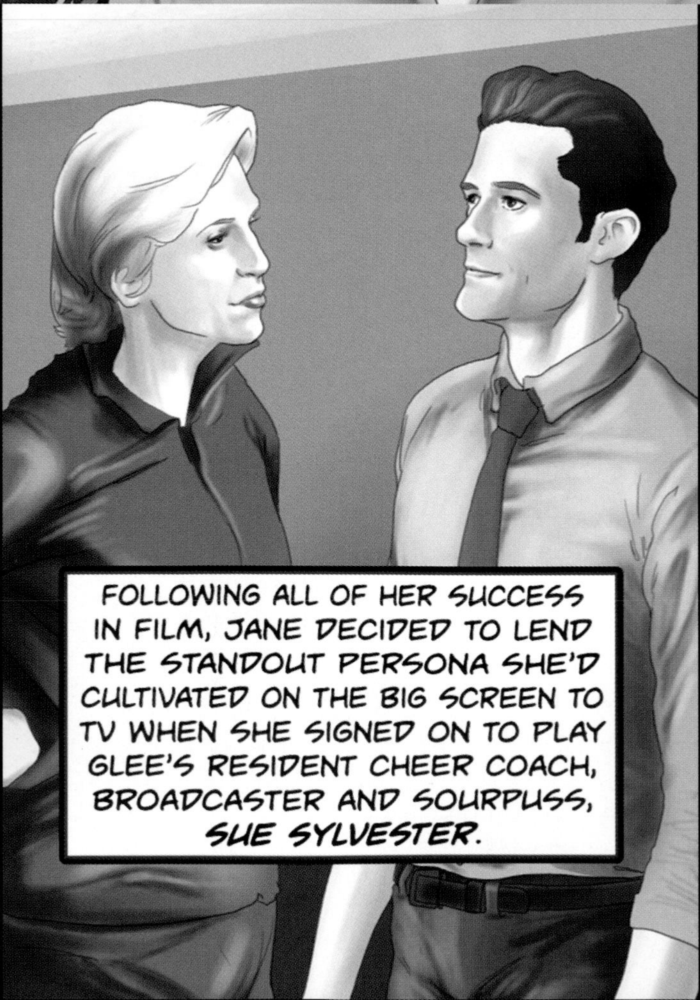
FOLLOWING ALL OF HER SUCCESS IN FILM, JANE DECIDED TO LEND THE STANDOUT PERSONA SHE'D CULTIVATED ON THE BIG SCREEN TO TV WHEN SHE SIGNED ON TO PLAY GLEE'S RESIDENT CHEER COACH, BROADCASTER AND SOURPUSS, SUE SYLVESTER.

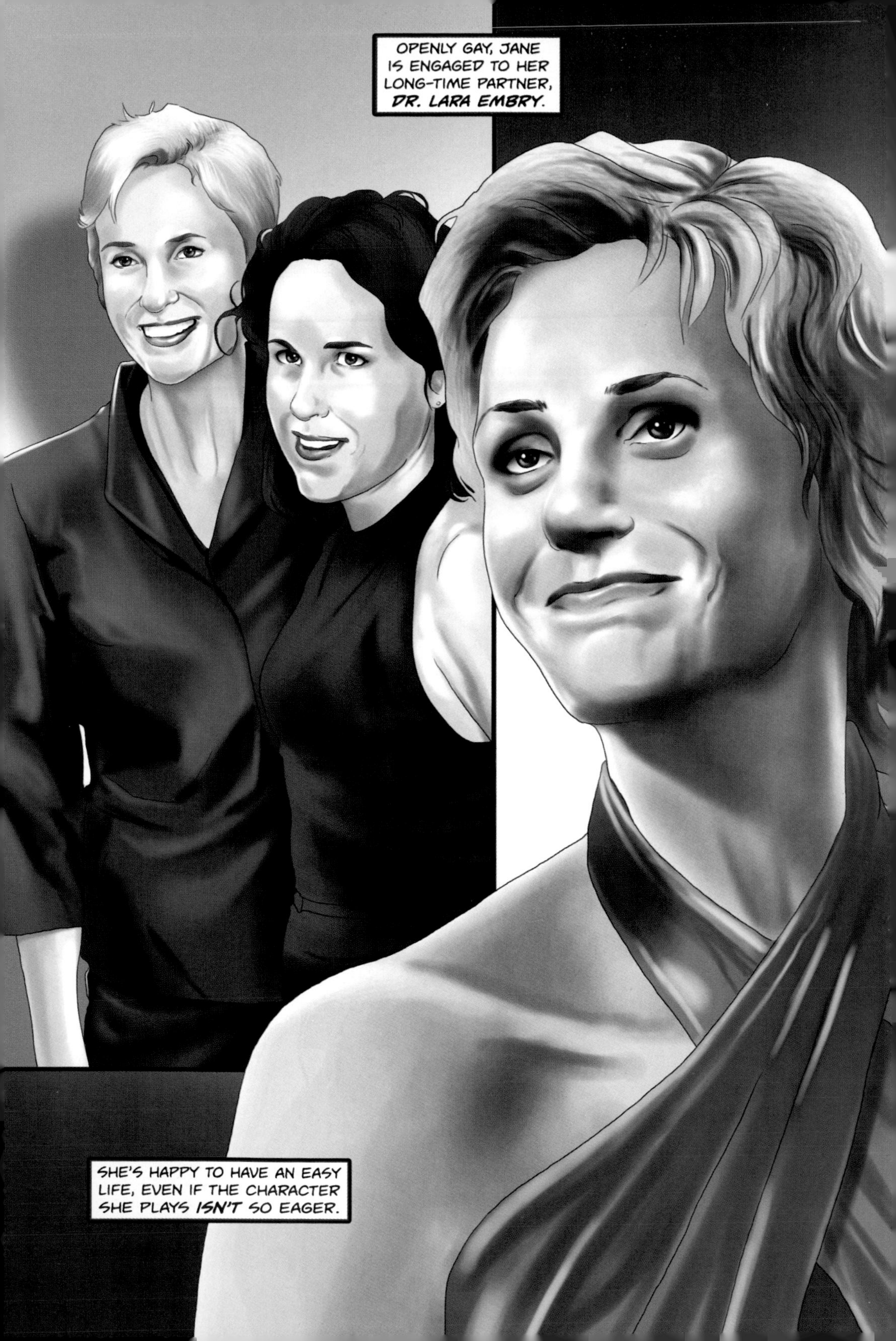
OPENLY GAY, JANE IS ENGAGED TO HER LONG-TIME PARTNER, DR. LARA EMBRY.
SHE'S HAPPY TO HAVE AN EASY LIFE, EVEN IF THE CHARACTER SHE PLAYS ISN'T SO EAGER.

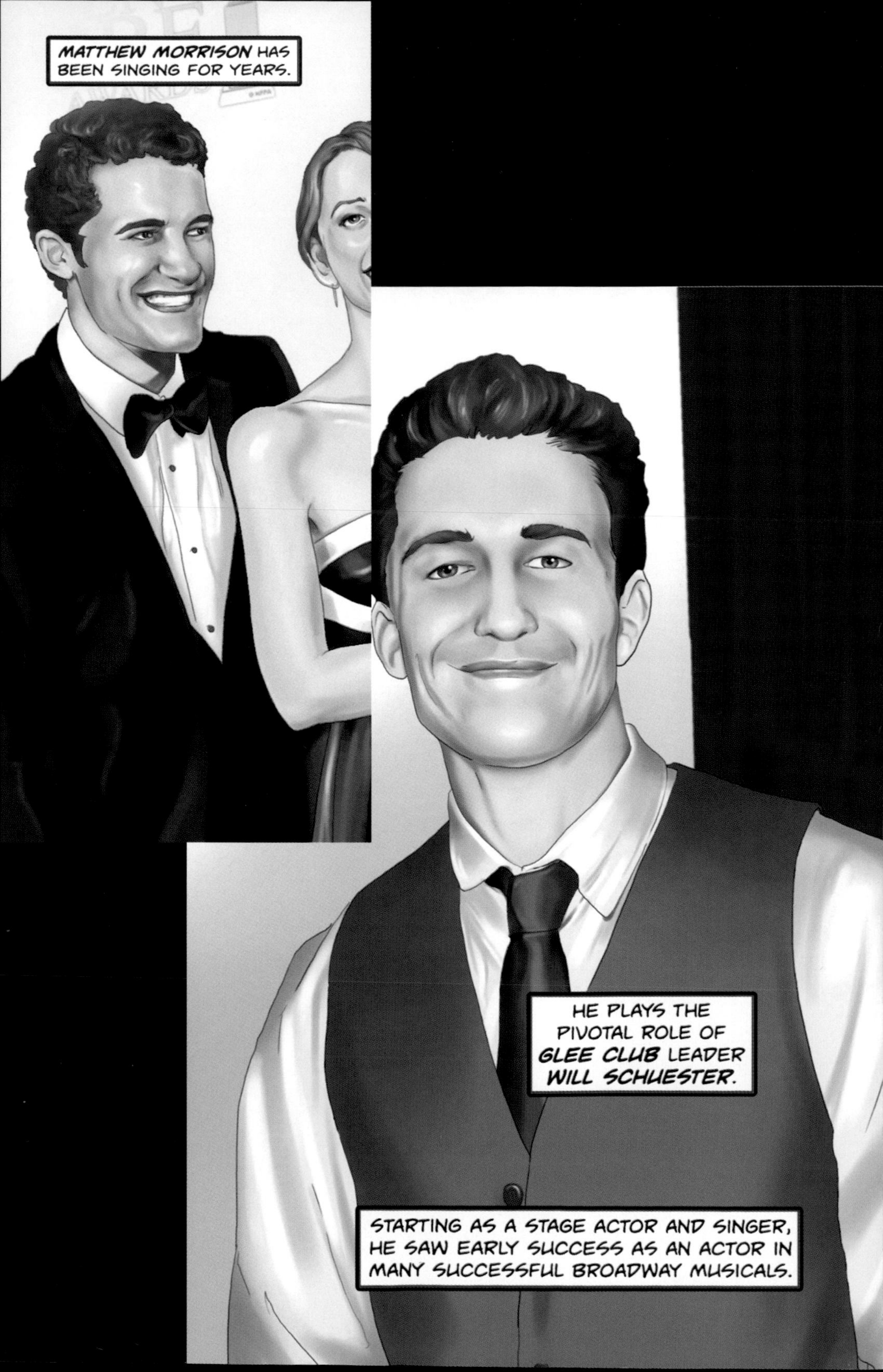
MATTHEW MORRISON HAS BEEN SINGING FOR YEARS.
HE PLAYS THE PIVOTAL ROLE OF GLEE CLUB LEADER WILL SCHUESTER.
STARTING AS A STAGE ACTOR AND SINGER, HE SAW EARLY SUCCESS AS AN ACTOR IN MANY SUCCESSFUL BROADWAY MUSICALS.

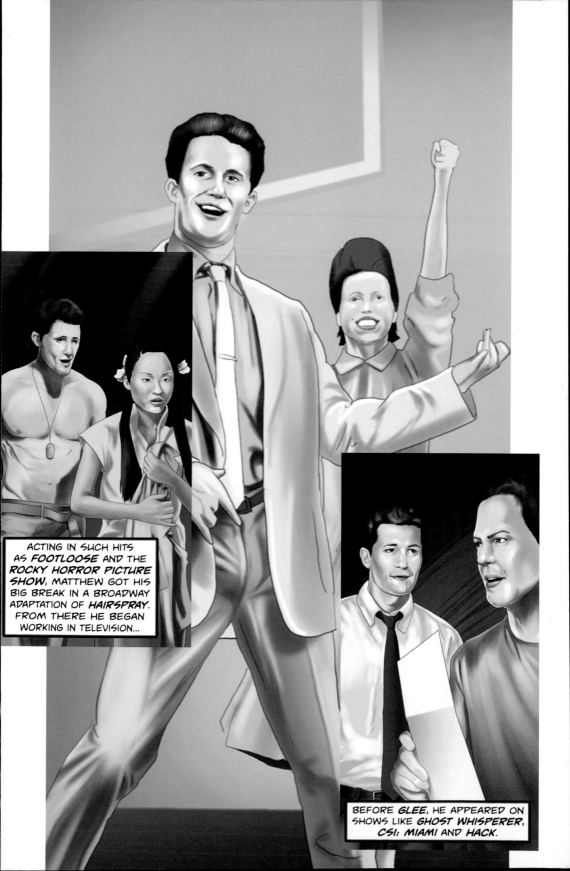

ACTING IN SUCH HITS
AS *FOOTLOOSE* AND THE
*ROCKY HORROR PICTURE
SHOW*, MATTHEW GOT HIS
BIG BREAK IN A BROADWAY
ADAPTATION OF *HAIRSPRAY*.
FROM THERE HE BEGAN
WORKING IN TELEVISION...

BEFORE *GLEE*, HE APPEARED ON
SHOWS LIKE *GHOST WHISPERER*,
CSI: MIAMI AND *HACK*.

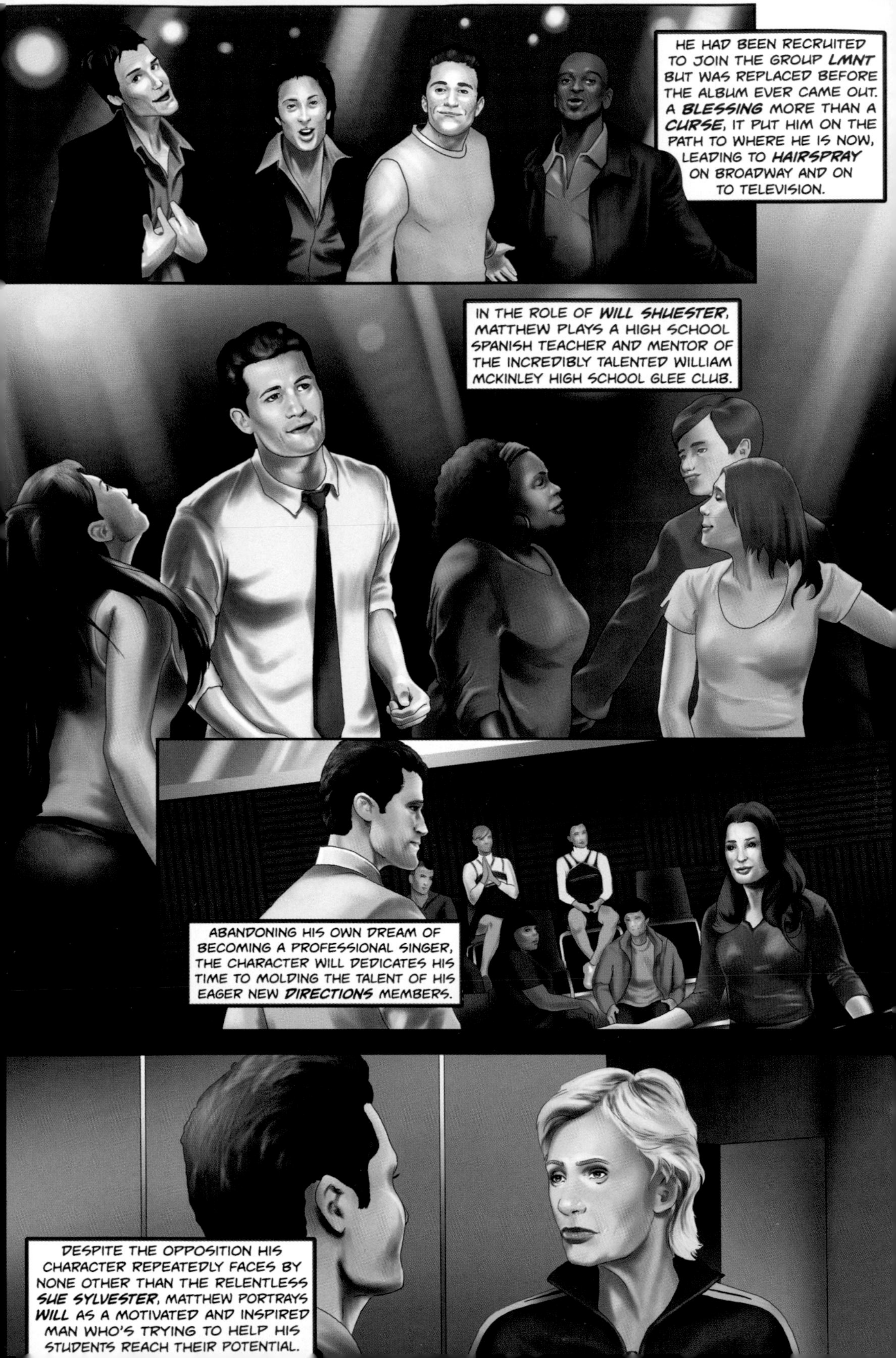
HE HAD BEEN RECRUITED TO JOIN THE GROUP LMNT BUT WAS REPLACED BEFORE THE ALBUM EVER CAME OUT. A BLESSING MORE THAN A CURSE, IT PUT HIM ON THE PATH TO WHERE HE IS NOW, LEADING TO HAIRSPRAY ON BROADWAY AND ON TO TELEVISION.
IN THE ROLE OF WILL SHUESTER, MATTHEW PLAYS A HIGH SCHOOL SPANISH TEACHER AND MENTOR OF THE INCREDIBLY TALENTED WILLIAM MCKINLEY HIGH SCHOOL GLEE CLUB.
ABANDONING HIS OWN DREAM OF BECOMING A PROFESSIONAL SINGER, THE CHARACTER WILL DEDICATES HIS TIME TO MOLDING THE TALENT OF HIS EAGER NEW DIRECTIONS MEMBERS.
DESPITE THE OPPOSITION HIS CHARACTER REPEATEDLY FACES BY NONE OTHER THAN THE RELENTLESS SUE SYLVESTER, MATTHEW PORTRAYS WILL AS A MOTIVATED AND INSPIRED MAN WHO'S TRYING TO HELP HIS STUDENTS REACH THEIR POTENTIAL.

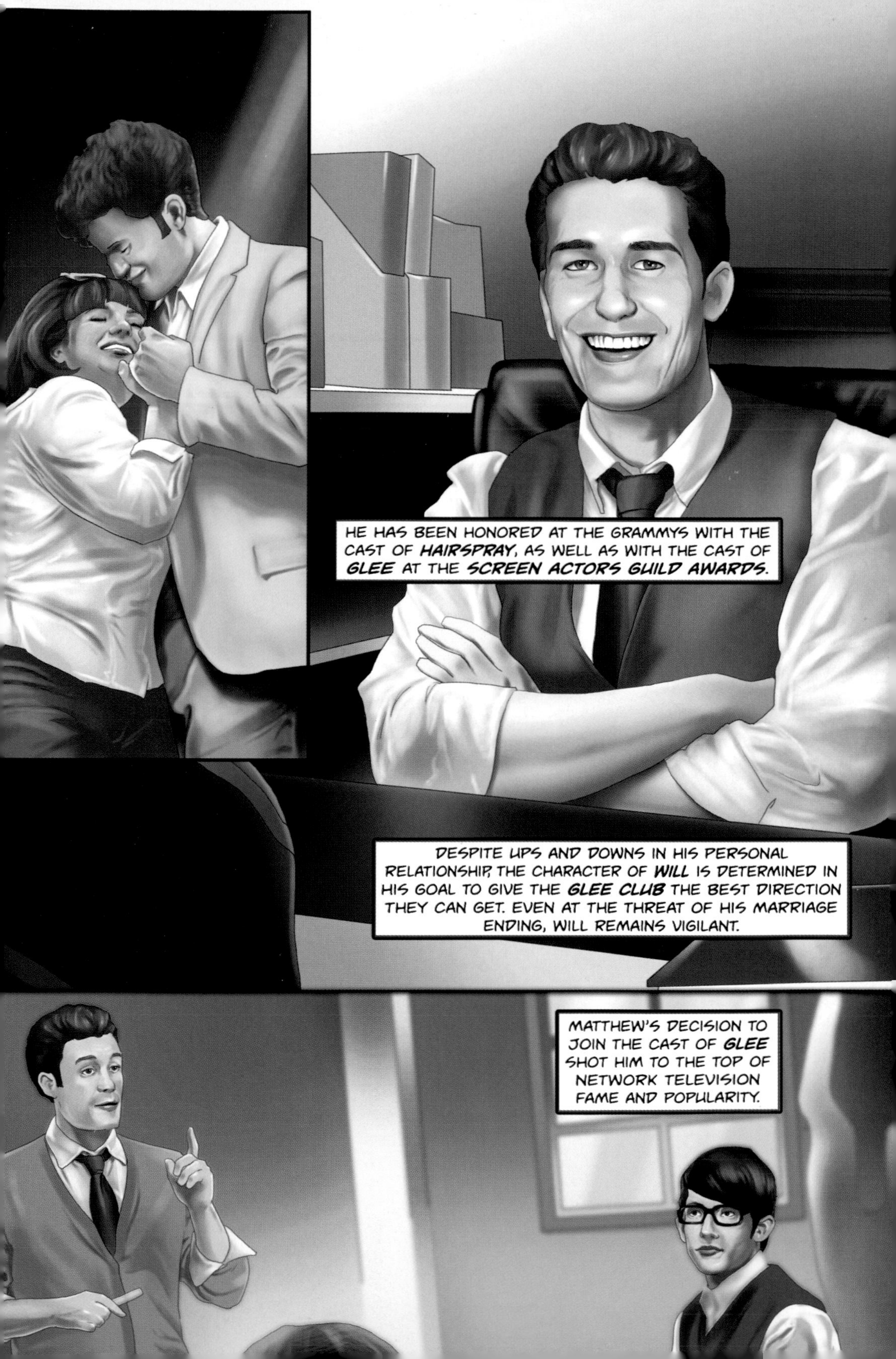
HE HAS BEEN HONORED AT THE GRAMMYS WITH THE CAST OF HAIRSPRAY, AS WELL AS WITH THE CAST OF GLEE AT THE SCREEN ACTORS GUILD AWARDS.
DESPITE UPS AND DOWNS IN HIS PERSONAL RELATIONSHIP, THE CHARACTER OF WILL IS DETERMINED IN HIS GOAL TO GIVE THE GLEE CLUB THE BEST DIRECTION THEY CAN GET. EVEN AT THE THREAT OF HIS MARRIAGE ENDING, WILL REMAINS VIGILANT.
MATTHEW'S DECISION TO JOIN THE CAST OF GLEE SHOT HIM TO THE TOP OF NETWORK TELEVISION FAME AND POPULARITY.

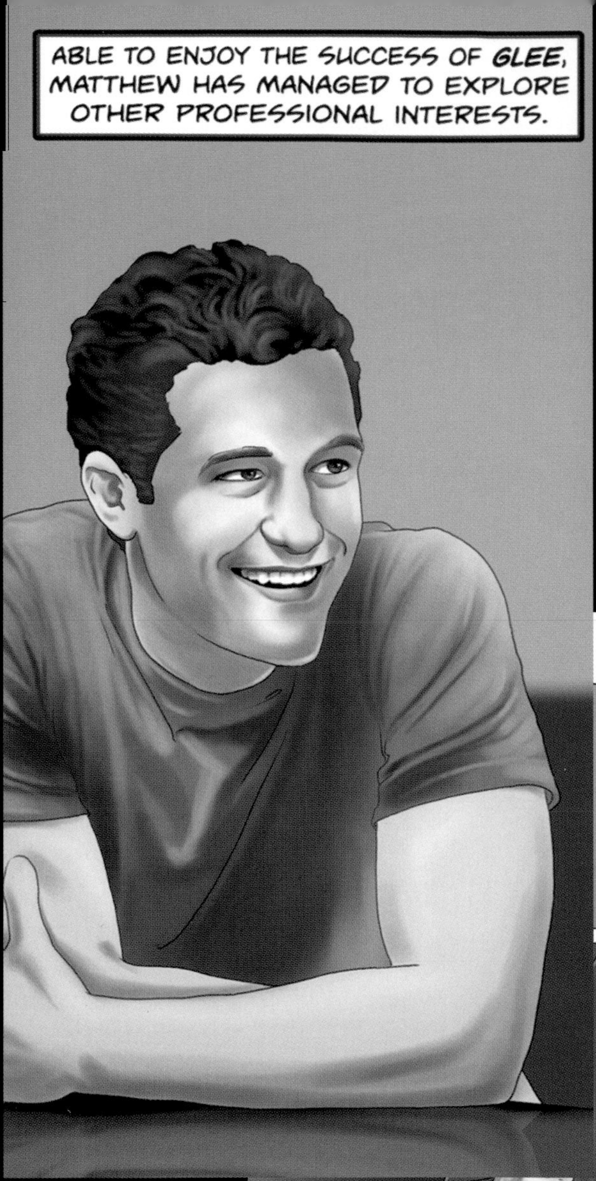
ABLE TO ENJOY THE SUCCESS OF *GLEE*, MATTHEW HAS MANAGED TO EXPLORE OTHER PROFESSIONAL INTERESTS.

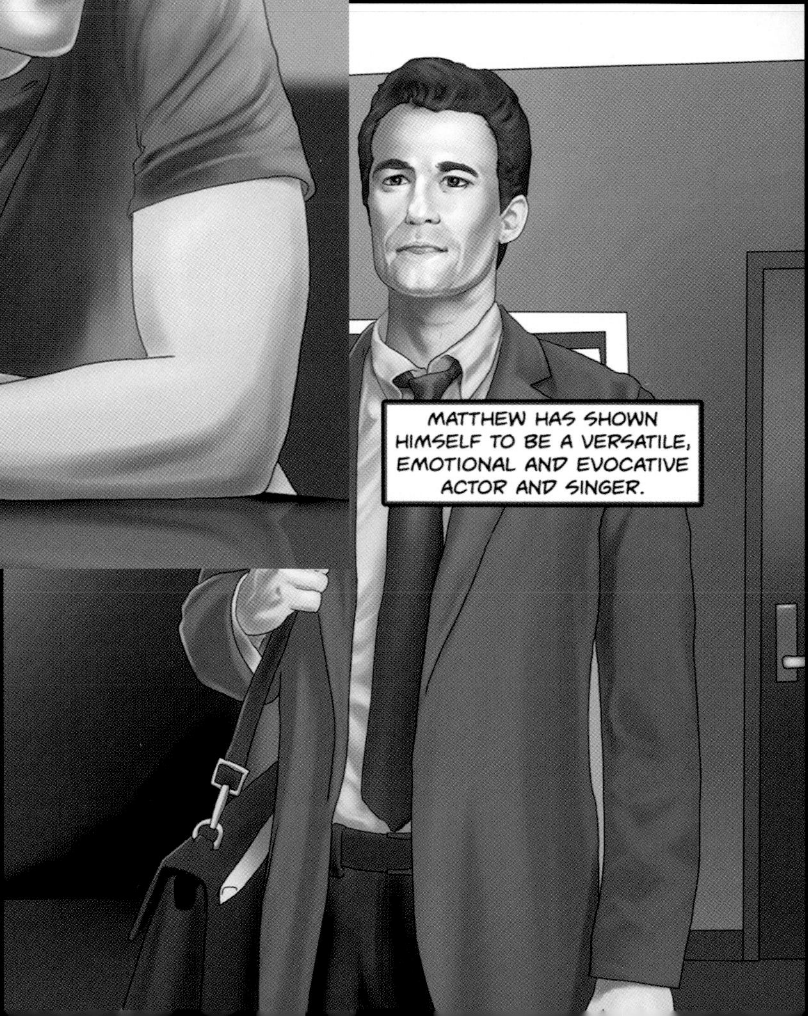
MATTHEW HAS SHOWN HIMSELF TO BE A VERSATILE, EMOTIONAL AND EVOCATIVE ACTOR AND SINGER.

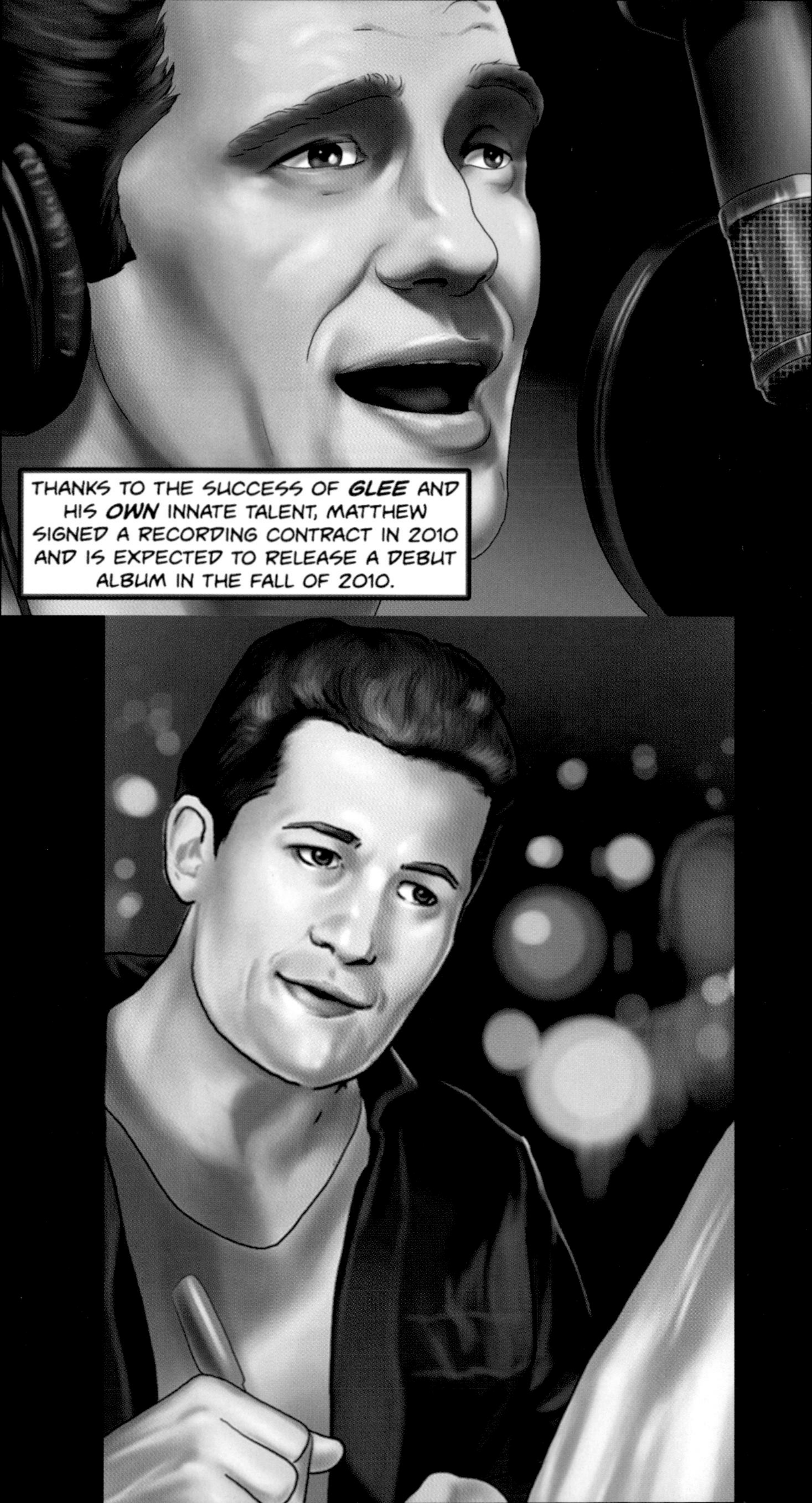
THANKS TO THE SUCCESS OF GLEE AND HIS OWN INNATE TALENT, MATTHEW SIGNED A RECORDING CONTRACT IN 2010 AND IS EXPECTED TO RELEASE A DEBUT ALBUM IN THE FALL OF 2010.

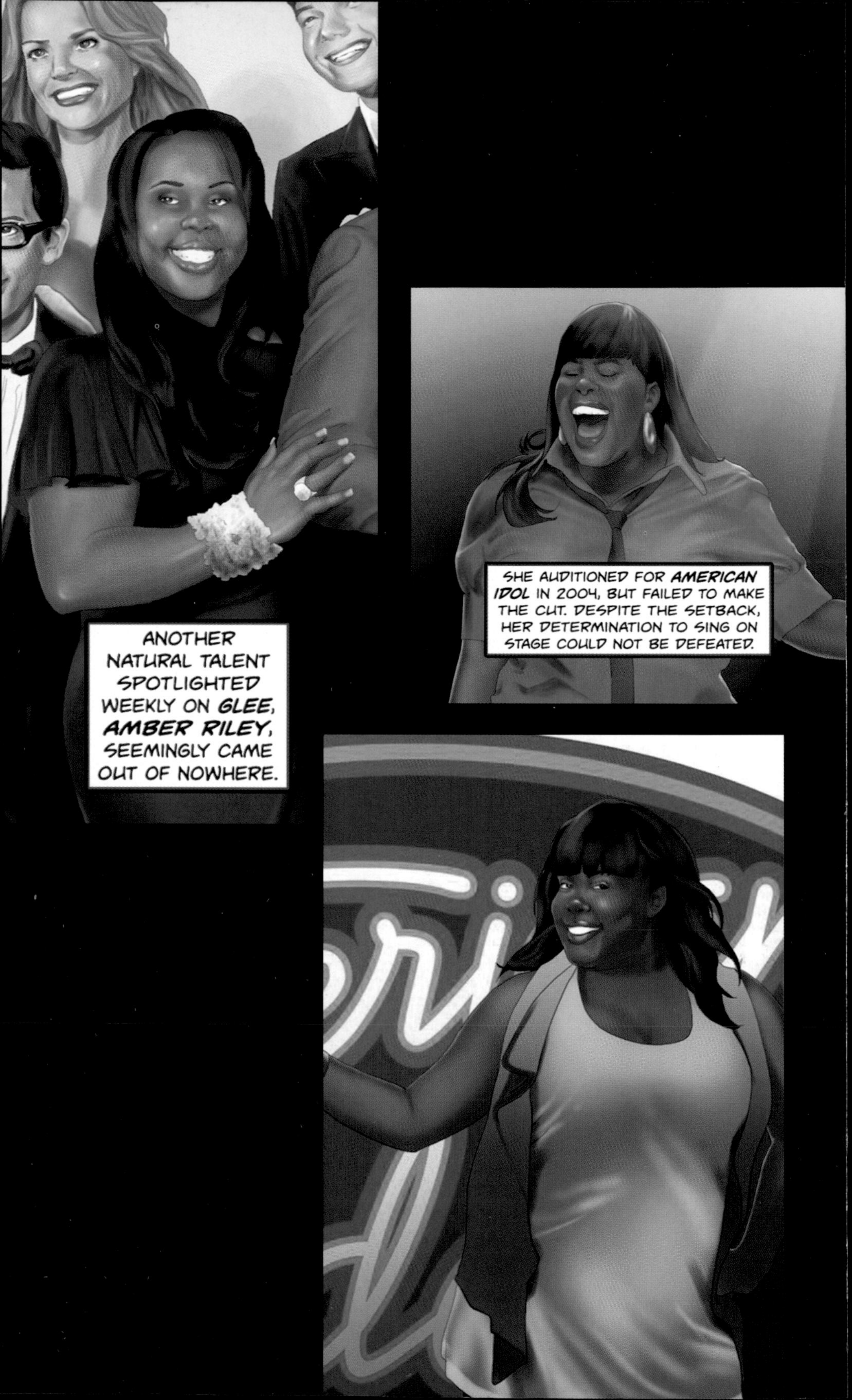
ANOTHER NATURAL TALENT SPOTLIGHTED WEEKLY ON GLEE, AMBER RILEY, SEEMINGLY CAME OUT OF NOWHERE.
SHE AUDITIONED FOR AMERICAN IDOL IN 2004, BUT FAILED TO MAKE THE CUT. DESPITE THE SETBACK, HER DETERMINATION TO SING ON STAGE COULD NOT BE DEFEATED.

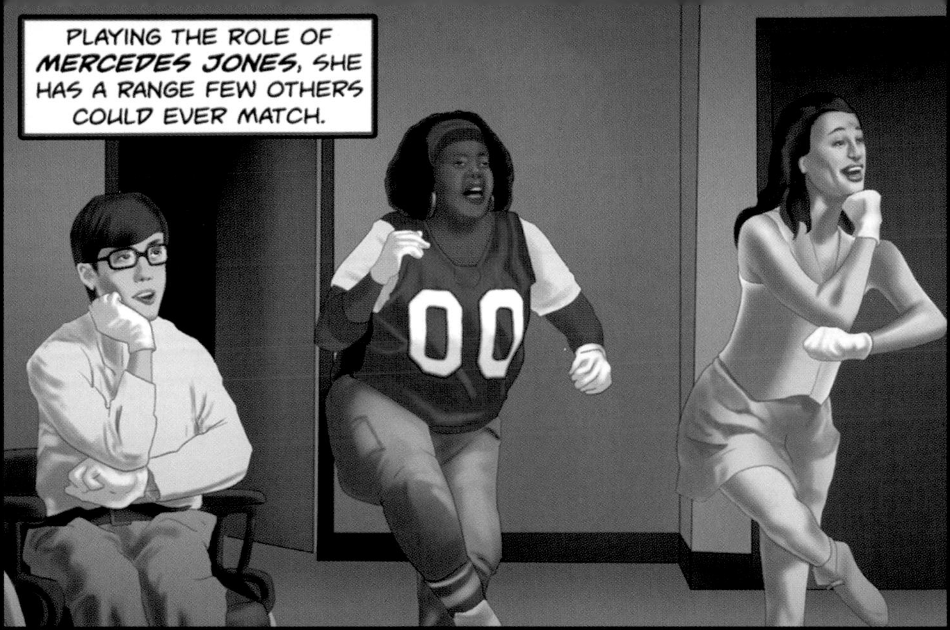
PLAYING THE ROLE OF ***MERCEDES JONES***, SHE HAS A RANGE FEW OTHERS COULD EVER MATCH.

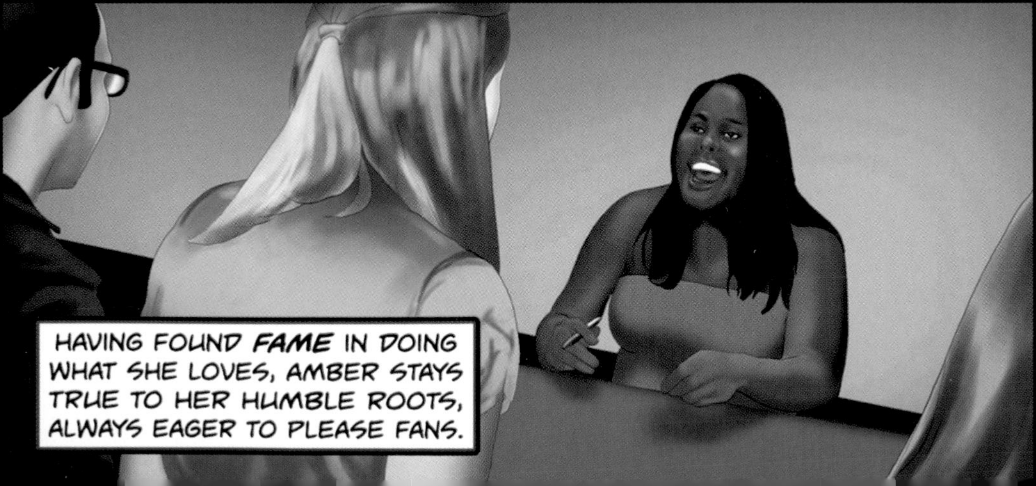
HAVING FOUND ***FAME*** IN DOING WHAT SHE LOVES, AMBER STAYS TRUE TO HER HUMBLE ROOTS, ALWAYS EAGER TO PLEASE FANS.

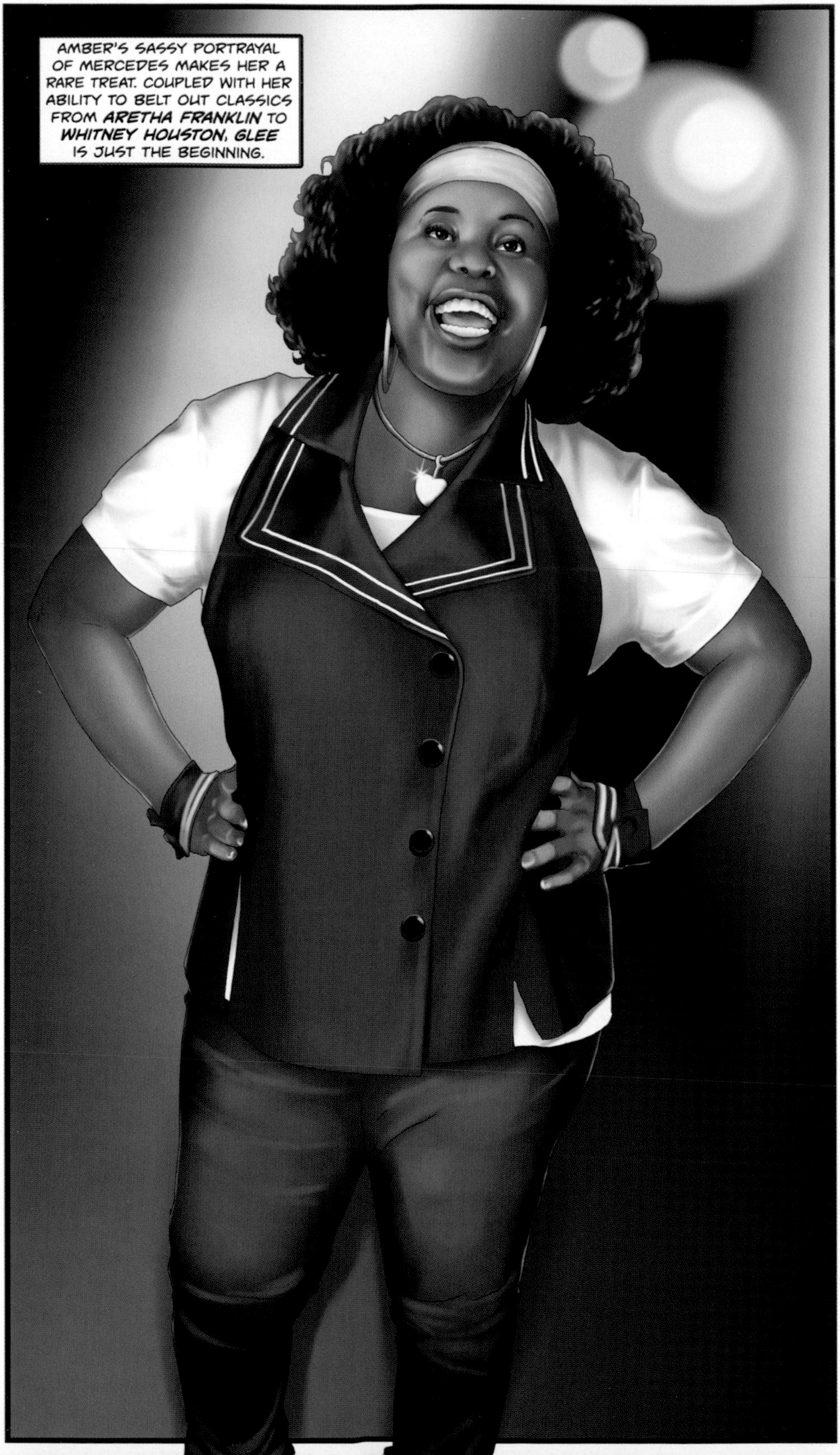
AMBER'S SASSY PORTRAYAL OF MERCEDES MAKES HER A RARE TREAT. COUPLED WITH HER ABILITY TO BELT OUT CLASSICS FROM ARETHA FRANKLIN TO WHITNEY HOUSTON, GLEE IS JUST THE BEGINNING.

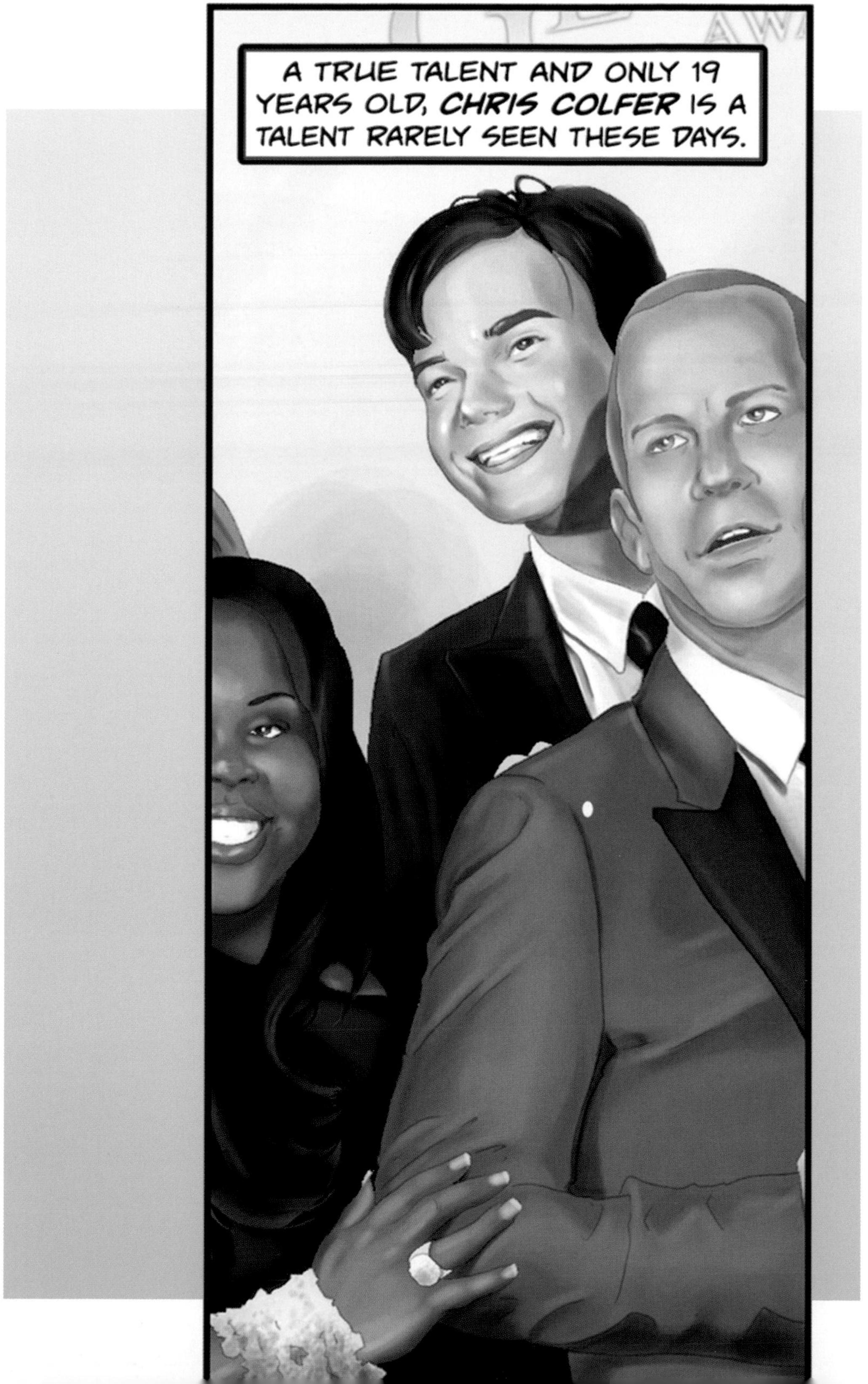
A TRUE TALENT AND ONLY 19 YEARS OLD, *CHRIS COLFER* IS A TALENT RARELY SEEN THESE DAYS.

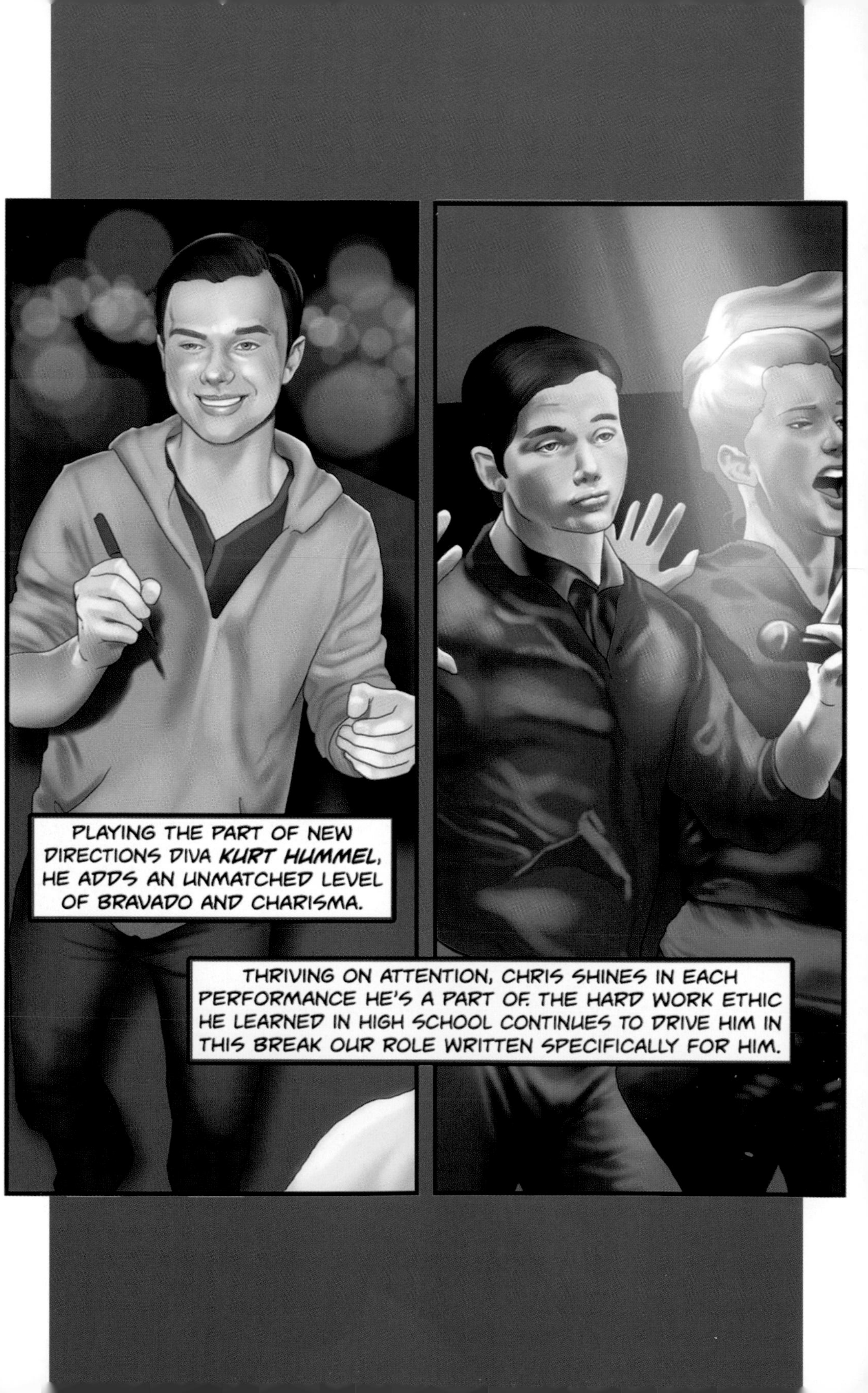
PLAYING THE PART OF NEW DIRECTIONS DIVA KURT HUMMEL, HE ADDS AN UNMATCHED LEVEL OF BRAVADO AND CHARISMA.
THRIVING ON ATTENTION, CHRIS SHINES IN EACH PERFORMANCE HE'S A PART OF. THE HARD WORK ETHIC HE LEARNED IN HIGH SCHOOL CONTINUES TO DRIVE HIM IN THIS BREAK OUR ROLE WRITTEN SPECIFICALLY FOR HIM.

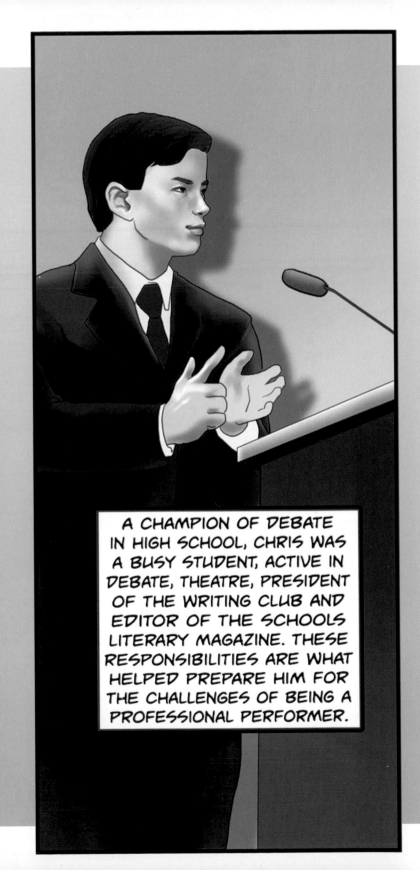

A CHAMPION OF DEBATE IN HIGH SCHOOL, CHRIS WAS A BUSY STUDENT, ACTIVE IN DEBATE, THEATRE, PRESIDENT OF THE WRITING CLUB AND EDITOR OF THE SCHOOLS LITERARY MAGAZINE. THESE RESPONSIBILITIES ARE WHAT HELPED PREPARE HIM FOR THE CHALLENGES OF BEING A PROFESSIONAL PERFORMER.

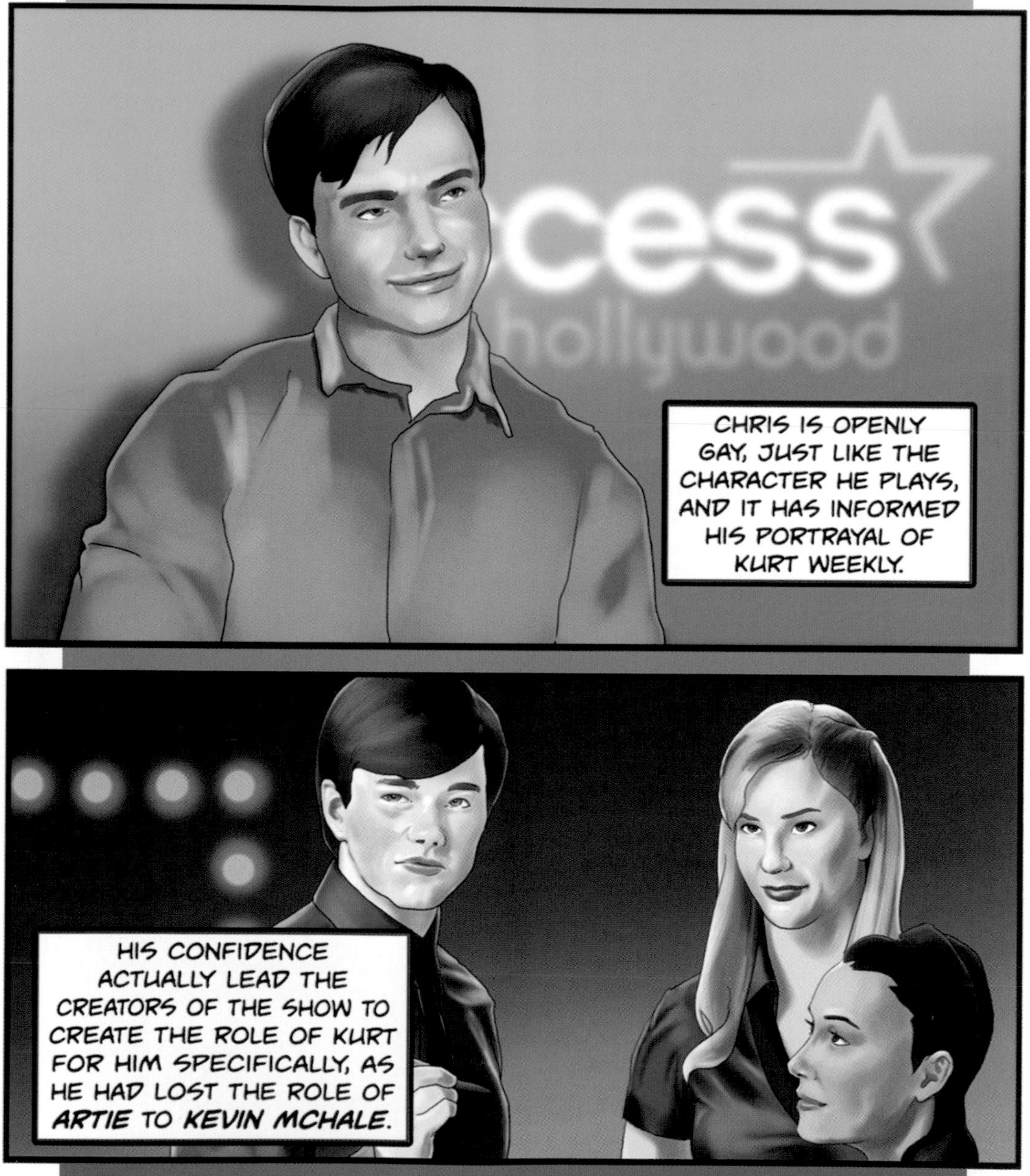
cess
hollywood
CHRIS IS OPENLY GAY, JUST LIKE THE CHARACTER HE PLAYS, AND IT HAS INFORMED HIS PORTRAYAL OF KURT WEEKLY.
HIS CONFIDENCE ACTUALLY LEAD THE CREATORS OF THE SHOW TO CREATE THE ROLE OF KURT FOR HIM SPECIFICALLY, AS HE HAD LOST THE ROLE OF ***ARTIE*** TO ***KEVIN MCHALE***.

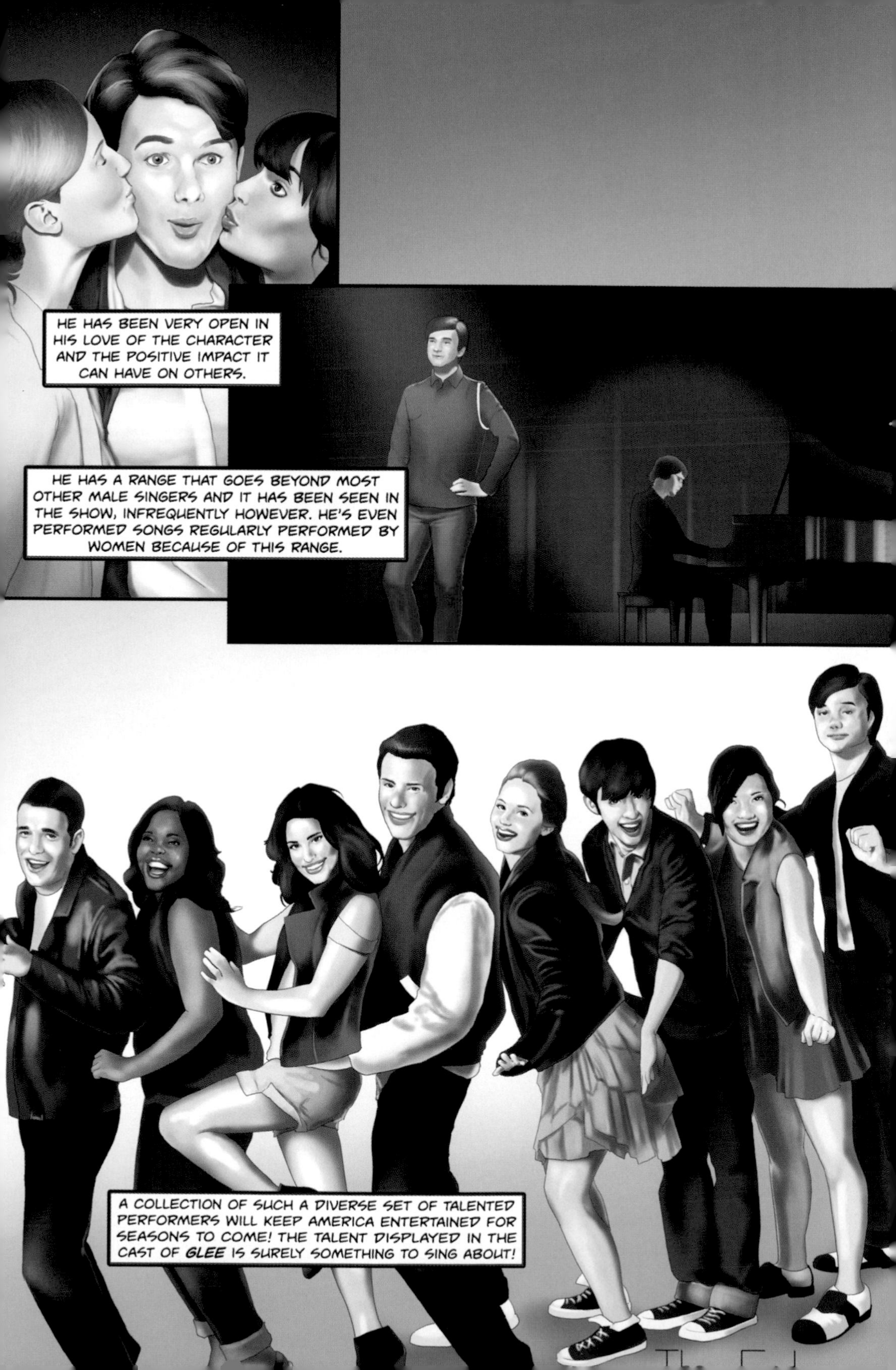
HE HAS BEEN VERY OPEN IN HIS LOVE OF THE CHARACTER AND THE POSITIVE IMPACT IT CAN HAVE ON OTHERS.
HE HAS A RANGE THAT GOES BEYOND MOST OTHER MALE SINGERS AND IT HAS BEEN SEEN IN THE SHOW, INFREQUENTLY HOWEVER. HE'S EVEN PERFORMED SONGS REGULARLY PERFORMED BY WOMEN BECAUSE OF THIS RANGE.
A COLLECTION OF SUCH A DIVERSE SET OF TALENTED PERFORMERS WILL KEEP AMERICA ENTERTAINED FOR SEASONS TO COME! THE TALENT DISPLAYED IN THE CAST OF **GLEE** IS SURELY SOMETHING TO SING ABOUT!

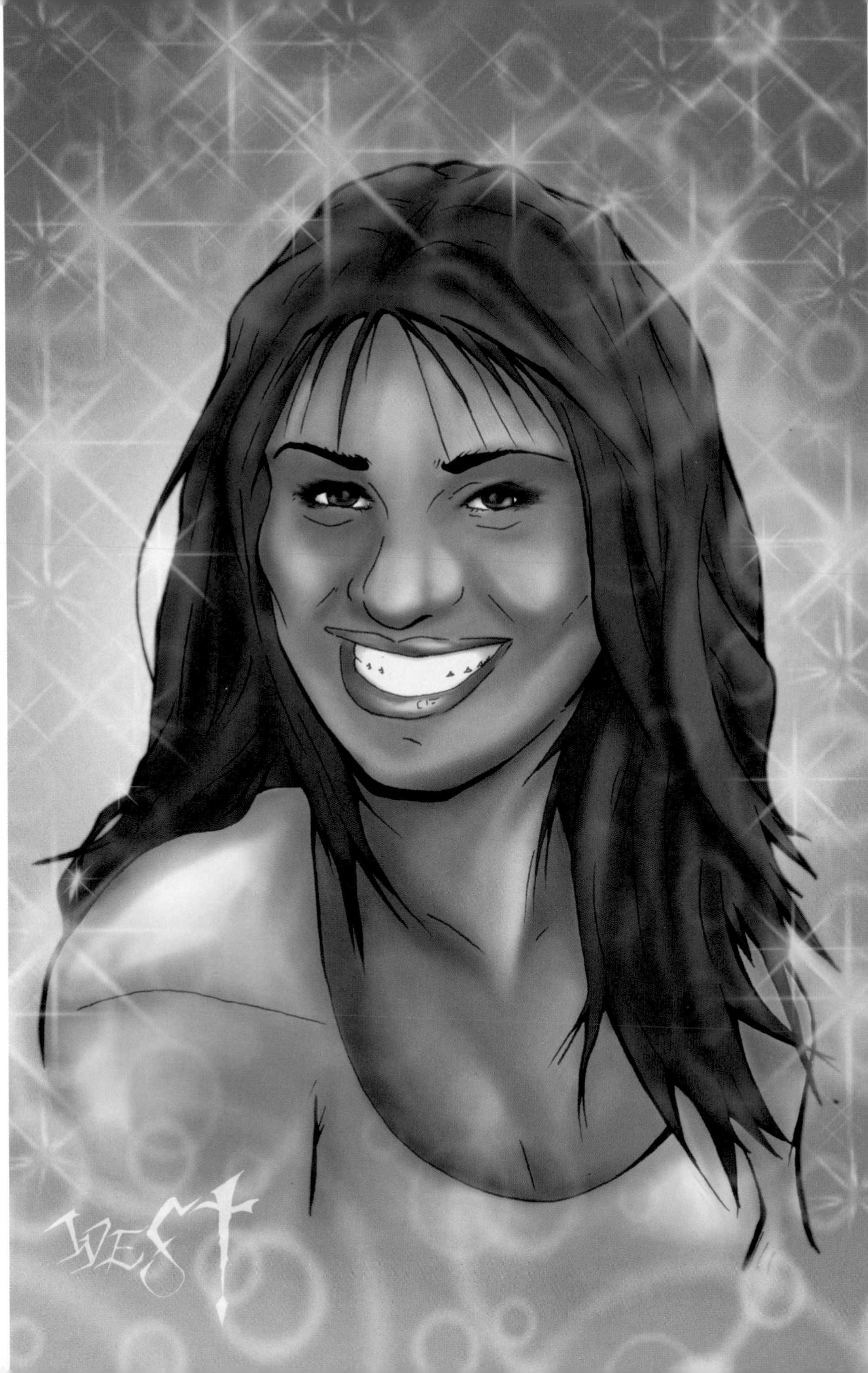
WEST

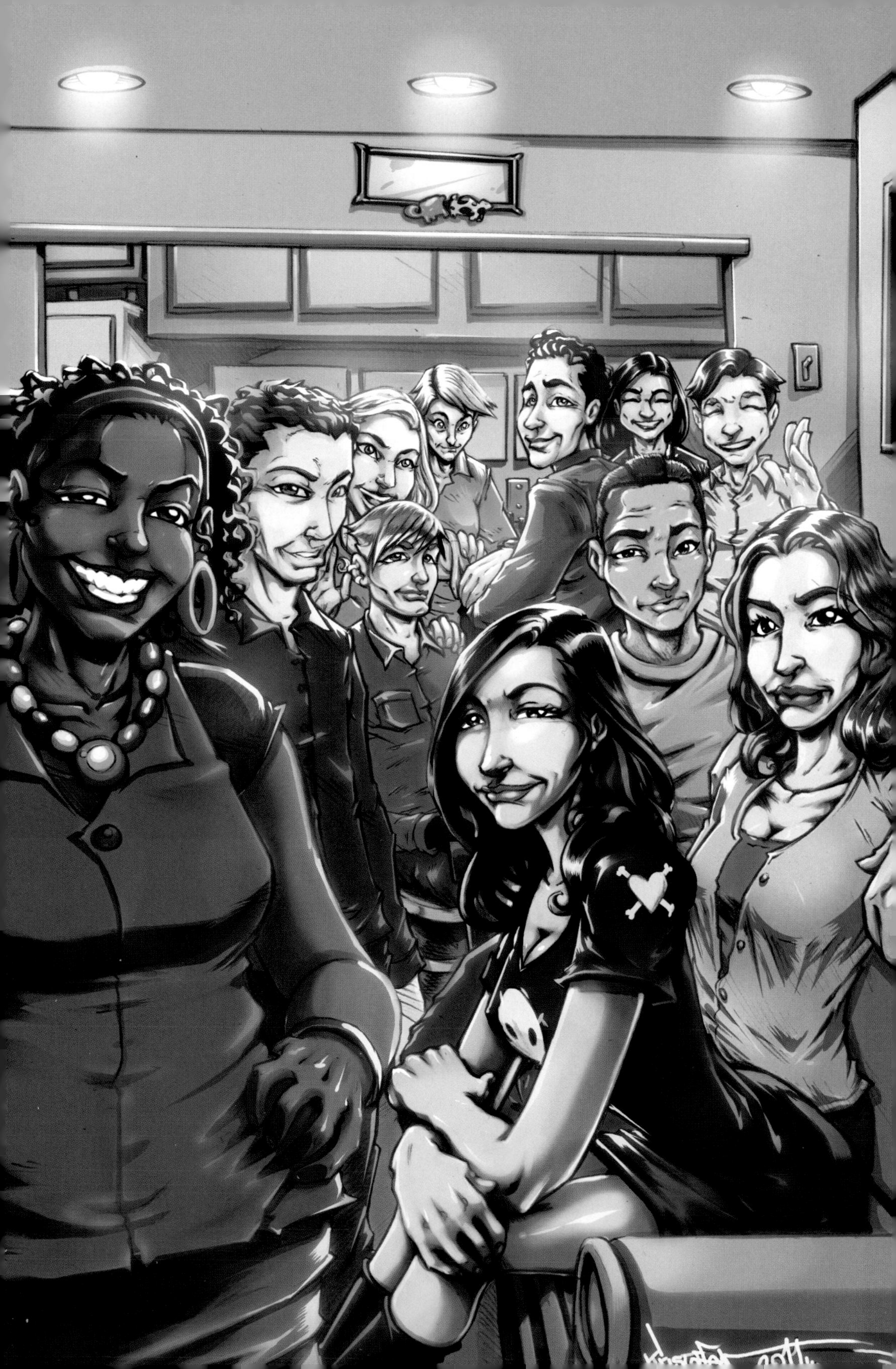

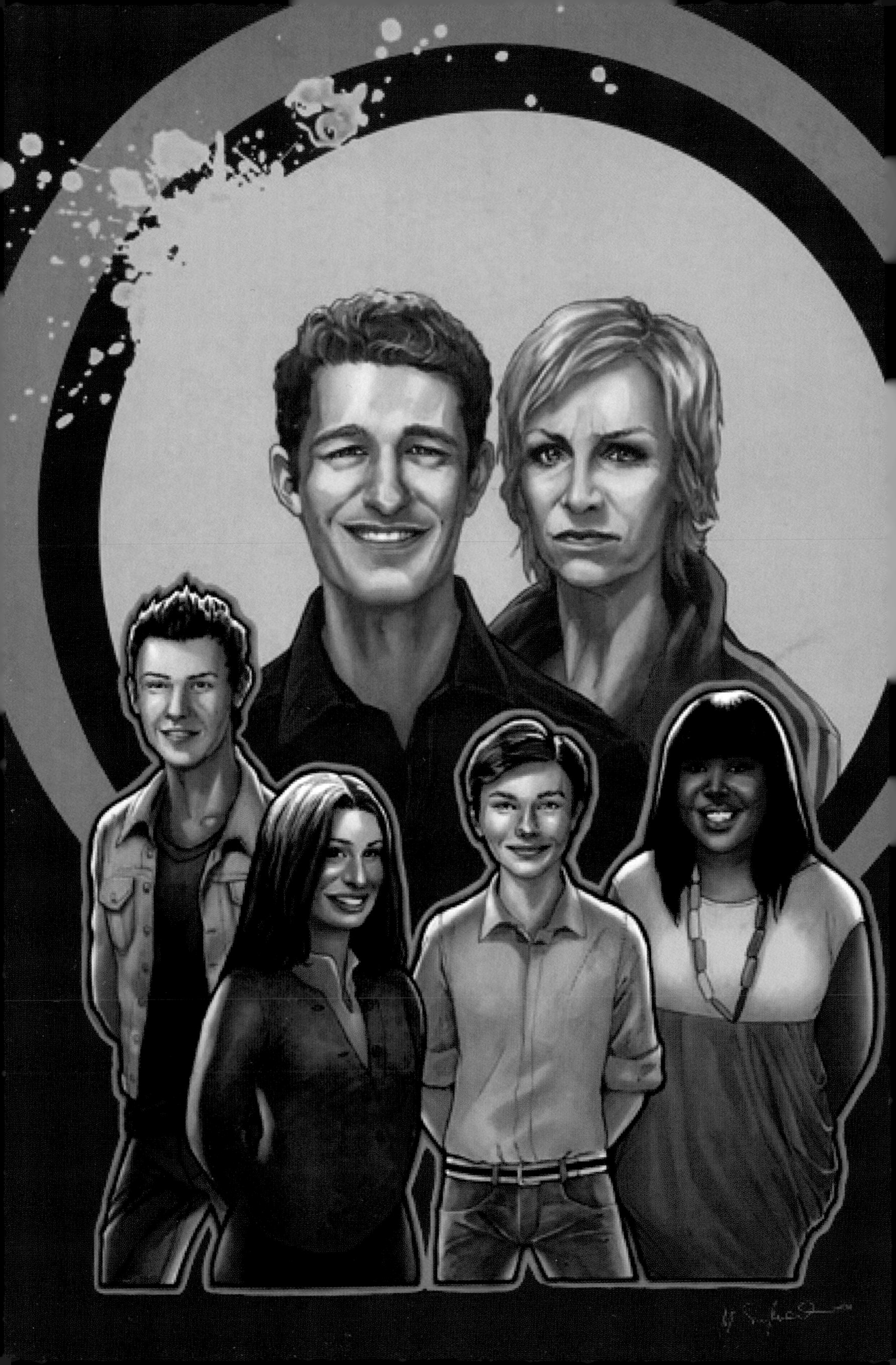

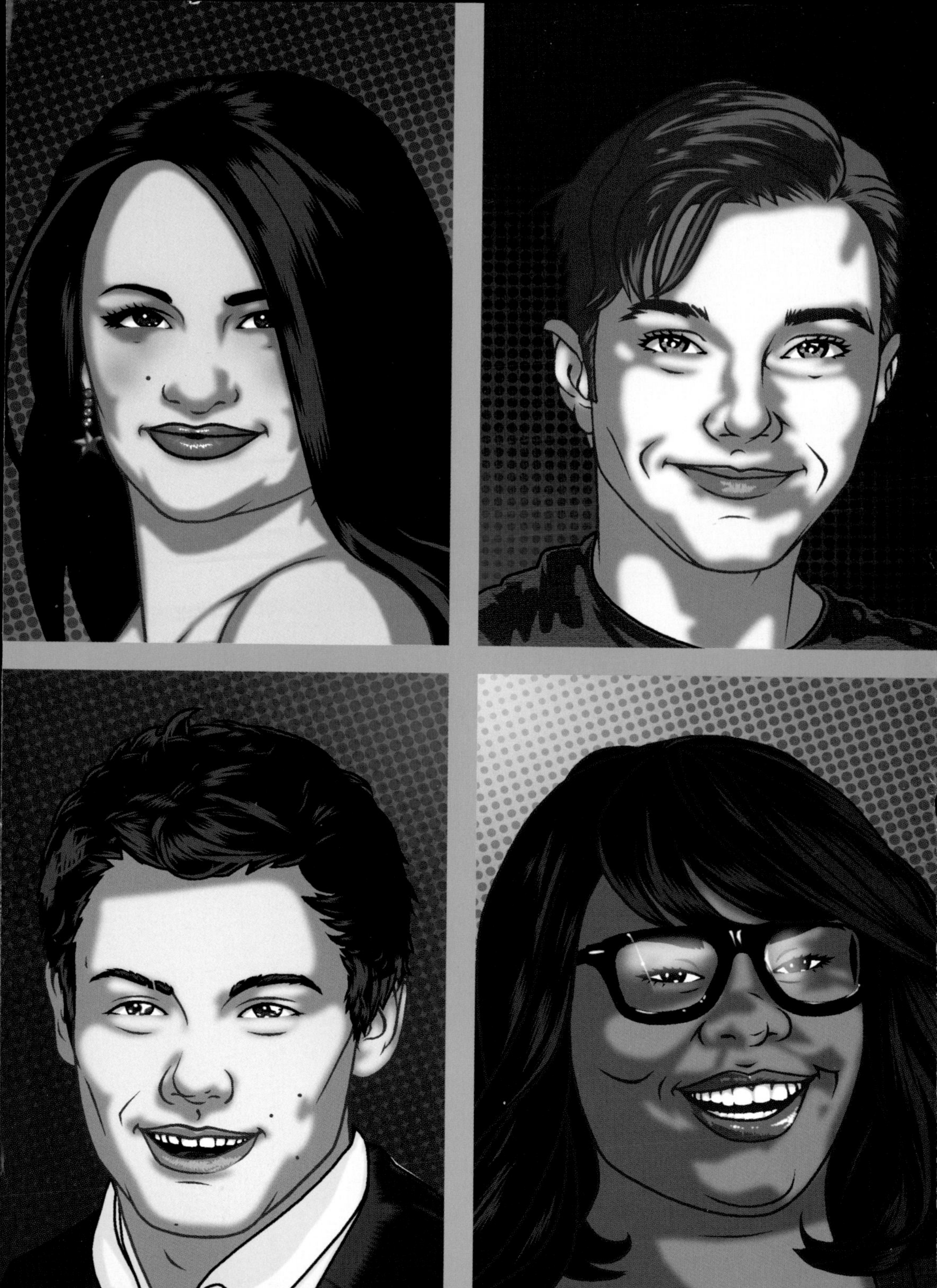

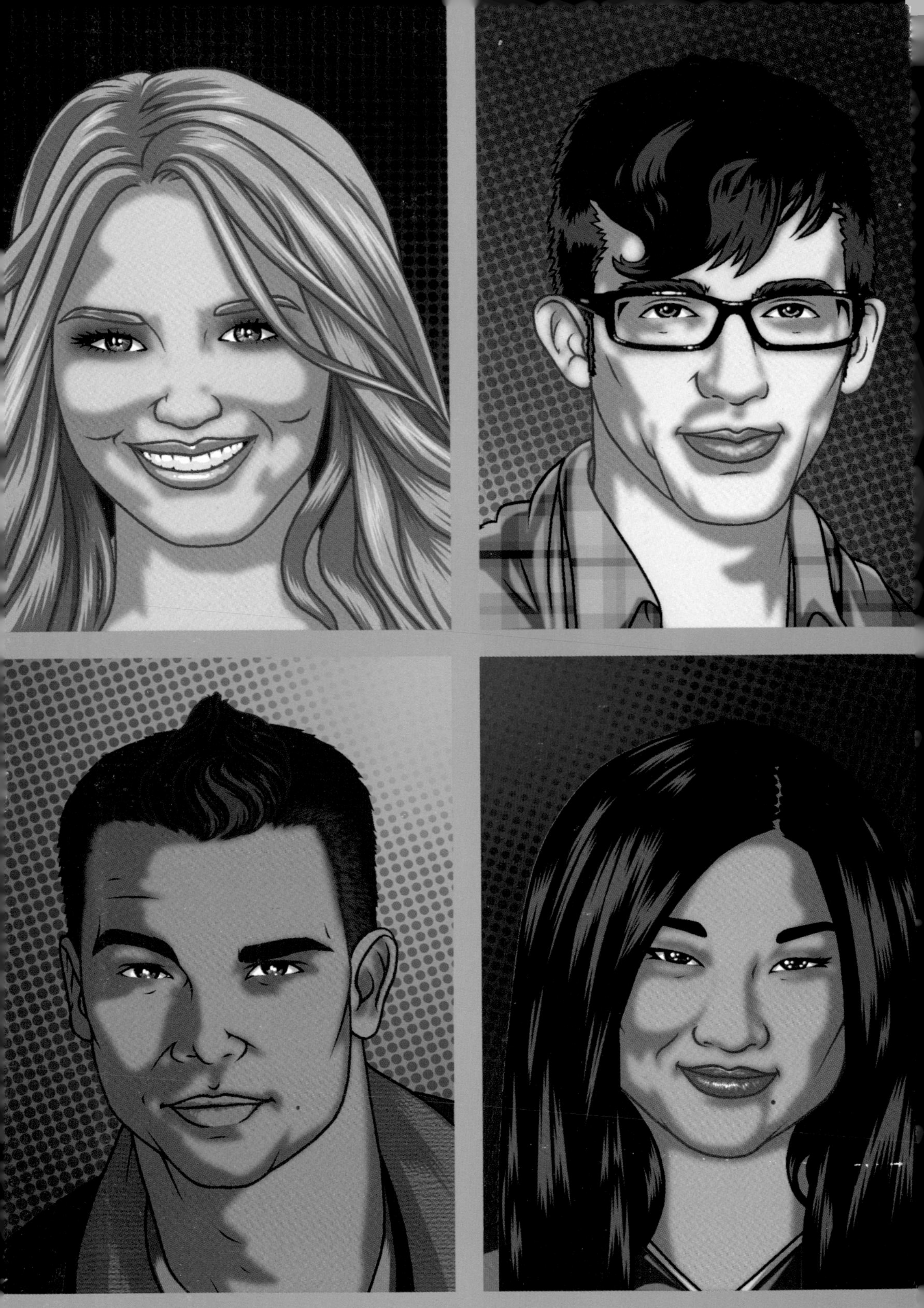